Utility Power Steadiness Evaluation using Transmission Circuit Enhancement Technologies

Adon HaKahal

Utility Power Steadiness Evaluation using Transmission Circuit Enhancement Technologies

First Edition June 2025

Written by Adon HaKahal

TABLE OF CONTENTS

CHAPTER NO.	TITLE	PAGE NO.

CHAPTER NO.	TITLE	PAGE NO.

CHAPTER NO.	TITLE	PAGE NO.

CHAPTER NO.	TITLE	PAGE NO.

CHAPTER NO.	TITLE	PAGE NO.

LIST OF TABLES

TABLE NO.	TITLE	PAGE NO.

LIST OF FIGURES

FIGURE NO.	TITLE	PAGE NO.

LIST OF ABBREVIATIONS

AC	-	Alternating Current
ACO	-	Ant Colony Optimization
ANN	-	Artificial Neural Network
AVR	-	Automatic Voltage Regulator
BFO	-	Bacterial Foraging Optimization
CPSS	-	Conventional Power System Stabilizer
DC	-	Direct Current
DE	-	Differential Evaluation
DFIG	-	Doubly Fed Induction Generator
DTC	-	Direct Torque Control
EA	-	Evolutionary Algorithm
EAC	-	Equal Area Criterion
EMS	-	Energy Management System
EP	-	Evolutionary Programming
ES	-	Evolutionary Strategies
FACTS	-	Flexible Alternating Current Transmission System
FLC	-	Fuzzy Logic Controller
F_{SHED}	-	Scheduled Frequency
GA	-	Genetic Algorithm
GH	-	Generic Heuristic
GSC	-	Grid Side Converters
HCC	-	Hybrid Coordinated Controller
HVDC	-	High Voltage Direct Current
ISO	-	Independent System Operation
MMCO	-	Modeling of Multi machine Controller Optimization

MMPSC	-	Multi Machine Power System Controller
MW	-	Mega Watt
NETS	-	New England Test System
NYPS	-	New York Power System
PCC	-	Point of Common Coupling
PD	-	Proportional Derivative
PF	-	Power Factor
P_G	-	Real Power
PI	-	Proportional Integral
PID	-	Proportional Integral Derivative
PMU	-	Phasor Measurement Units
POD	-	Power Oscillation Damper
P_{SHED}	-	Scheduled Power
PSO	-	Particle Swarm Optimization
PSS	-	Power System Stabilizer
PWM	-	Pulse With Modulation
RSC	-	Rotor Side Converters
SCADA	-	Supervisory Control and Data Acquisition
SM	-	Synchronous Motors
SMIB	-	Single Machine Infinite Bus System
SP	-	Set Point
STATCOM	-	Static Synchronous Compensator
SVC	-	Static Volt ampere reactive Compensator
SVD	-	Singular Value Decomposition
THD	-	Total Harmonic Distortion
VAR	-	Volt Ampere Reactive
V_G	-	Generator Voltage
V_{REF}	-	Reference Voltage
WT	-	Wind Turbine

CHAPTER 1

INTRODUCTION

1.1 POWER SYSTEM OVERVIEW

Numerous methods of electrification due to scientific improvement have shown the way to continuous development and growth of the electric power system over the last hundred years. The recent electric power system is responsible for generation, transmission and distribution of energy sources. Due to this widespread growth, the complication and issues in the electric power system has developed to a superior level. To overcome the issues in the electric power system, a new innovative controller has to be designed and stabilized the complex system. Several computer aided tools are used to evaluate the features of monitoring, control and operation functions. The computer based monitoring technology such as Control Centres, Energy Management Systems (EMS), Independent System Operations (ISO), etc. progressively improves the performance of the electric power systems. This research work focuses on improving the performance of the power system stability by using different controllers.

As discussed earlier, Generation, Transmission, and distribution are the main stages in Power systems. In the first stage, synchronous generators or Doubly Fed Induction Generator (DFIG) were used to generate the electric power. Then the transformer is used to reduce the line currents and power transmission losses in the transmission stage. Finally, the voltage is stepped down using transformers in order to be distributed accordingly.

Power systems are designed to provide continuous power supply that maintains voltage stability. However, due to undesired events such as accidents or any other unpredictable events like lightning , short circuits between the phase wires of the transmission lines or between a phase wire and the ground which may occur is called a fault. Due to occurring of a fault, some of the generators may be harshly disturbed causing an inequality among generation and demand. In case the fault holds for and is not cleared in a pre-shown time traverse, it may achieve genuine damages to the rigging which in this manner may incite to an influence mishap and impact power outage. Therefore, protective equipment are installed to detect faults and clear/isolate faulted parts of the power system as quickly as possible before the fault energy is propagated to the rest of the system.

1.2 POWER SYSTEM STABILITY PROBLEM

Power system stability is a major problem in order to supply continuous power to the applications. The stability of a power system is portrayed as property to keep up a condition of operating harmony under ordinary working conditions and to recuperate a satisfactory condition of balance in the wake of being subjected to an unsettling influence. Instability of power system can occur in many different situations depending on the system configuration and operating mode. The stability problems mainly include the problem of synchronous operation of power system machines during generation. This aspect is influenced by the dynamic of generator rotor angles and power-angle relationships. Other instability problem that may be encountered is voltage collapse that is mostly related to load behaviour and not synchronous speed of generators.

1.3 FORMS OF POWER SYSTEM INSTABILITY

There are three different forms of power system instability: rotor angle instability, voltage instability and voltage collapse, and mid-term and long-term instability. Rotor angle stability is the ability of interconnected synchronous machines of a power system to remain in synchronism. Voltage stability is the ability of a power system to maintain acceptable voltages at all buses in the system under normal operating conditions and after being subjected to a disturbance. For the voltage to be stable, the synchronous machines must run in synchronism.

The long-term and mid-term stability are relatively new to the literature on power system stability. Long-term stability is associated with the slower and longer-duration phenomena that accompany large-scale system upsets and on the resulting large, and sustained mismatches between generation and consumption of active and reactive power. In mid-term stability, the focus is on synchronizing power oscillations between machines, including the effects of some of the slower phenomena and possibly large voltage or frequency excursions.

1.4 WHY POWER SYSTEM STABILITY

Power system stability is a complex subject that has challenged power system engineers for many years. Power systems operate closer and closer to their limits which makes the instability problem to be more probable. With that given, it is very important to detect any disturbance that may cause the instability. Instability may occur during steady-state however, it occurs more frequently following short-circuits which makes the time to clear a large disturbance to be very short. That is, it is very crucial to determine whether the system will be transient stable or will lose its synchronism. Therefore, transient stability analysis requires very fast computation and decision making.

1.5 HISTORICAL REVIEW OF POWER SYSTEM STABILITY PROBLEMS

Different forms of instability have emerged over the last century. The methods of power system stability problems analysis were influenced by the development of computational tools, stability theories, and power system control technologies. Therefore, it is very essential to present a review of the history of the subject to better understand the methods used in industries with regard of system stability and how these developments relate to the proposed practical method in the thesis.

Power system stability is a complex problem that has challenged power system engineers for many years. It was first recognized as an important problem in 1920s, Steinmetz (1920), Evans & Bergvall (1924) and Wilkins (1926). The first field tests on the stability on a practical power system were conducted in 1925. The early stability problems were associated with remote power plants feeding load centres over long transmission lines. With slow exciters and non-continuously acting voltage regulators, power transfer capability was often limited by steady-state as well as transient rotor angle instability due to insufficient synchronizing torque.

In the early years, graphical methods such as, Equal Area Criterion (EAC) and power circle diagrams were developed. These methods were successfully applied to early systems that could be represented as two-machine systems. As the systems become larger, and interconnection which was found to be economically better, the complexity of the systems grew and therefore the stability problems became more complex, which voided the treatment of the systems to be two-machine systems. A significant step towards the improvement of stability calculations was the development in 1930 of the network analyzer which was capable of power flow analysis of multi-machine power systems. A network analyzer is essentially a scaled model of an AC power system with adjustable resistors, inductors and capacitors to represent the transmission network and loads, voltage sources whose magnitude and angle are adjustable, and meters to measure voltages, currents, and power anywhere in the network. However, system dynamic still had to be solved by hand by solving the swing equations using step-by-step numerical integration. During this period, classical models were used for the swing equations; that is, by representing the generators by fixed transient reactance and a fixed power supply behind these reactance.

In the early 1950s, electronic analogy computers were used for analysis of special problems requiring detailed modelling of the synchronous machine, excitation system, and speed governor. Also, during that period, development of digital computers was seen, and specifically about 1956, the first digital program for power system stability analysis was developed. In the 1960s, most of the power systems in the United States and Canada were joined as part of one of two large interconnected systems, one in the east and the other in the west. In 1967, low capacity HVDC ties were also established between the east and west systems. Nowadays, the power systems in the United States and Canada form virtually one large system. This interconnection between the two systems result in operating economy and increased reliability, though, it increased the complexity of stability problems and increase the consequences of instability.

Until recently, most industry effort and interest has been concentrated on transient (rotor angle) stability. Powerful transient stability simulation programs have been developed that are capable of modelling large complex systems using detailed models. In the early 1990s, the focus was on small-signal stability which then led to the development of special study techniques, such as modal analysis using Eigen value techniques. In the 1970s and 1980s, frequency stability problems were experienced following major system upsets led to an investigation of the underlying causes of such problems and to the development of long-term dynamic simulation programs to assist in their analysis. In 1983, guidelines were developed for enhancing power plant response during major frequency disturbance.

From the history, it is clear that increased competition, transmission access, and environmental constraints are shaping the operation of electric power systems which present greater challenges for secure system operation. This is clear from the increasing number of major power-grid blackouts that have been experienced in recent years. Planning and operation of today's power systems require a careful consideration of all forms of system instability. Significant advances have been made in recent years in providing better tools and techniques to analyze instability in power systems.

1.6 POWER SYSTEM ORGANIZATION

The structure of power system mainly consists of three stages. The classified stages are Generation, Transmission and Distribution and Utilization.

Generation includes number of generators and transformers. Generators are essential components of power systems and the widely used generators are Alternating Current (AC) generator or synchronous generator. The slip rings in the machine are called as DC generators accommodated on the same shaft in the older machines. Contemporary machinery works based on DFIG generators with rectifiers and grid side inverter stages in the power systems. The DFIG based generator system sustains generator voltage and controls the reactive power flow.

Transmission stage defined as the transfer of power between regions during emergencies. Hence distribution of electric power from generating units to the delivery system which finally provides to the load.

Distribution system is used to distribute the service to the consumers. Distribution systems employ both overhead and underground conductors. The extensive development of underground distribution has been particularly quick and as much as 70 percent of new residential construction employs underground systems.

Utilization of electrical energy is partitioned into industrial, commercial and residential loads. Commercial and residential loads mostly comprise of lighting, heating and cooking. These loads are not dependent of frequency and utilize very little reactive power.

1.7 POWER SYSTEM CONTROL FUNCTIONS

The functioning of an electric power system is characterized with a number of control functions. Some of them are automatic and others need operator initiation. For instance, a single unit power plant shown in Figure 1.1 is considered and a number of control loops are present. They are voltage control loop, power system stabilizer loop, primary automatic generator control loop and secondary automatic generation control loop.

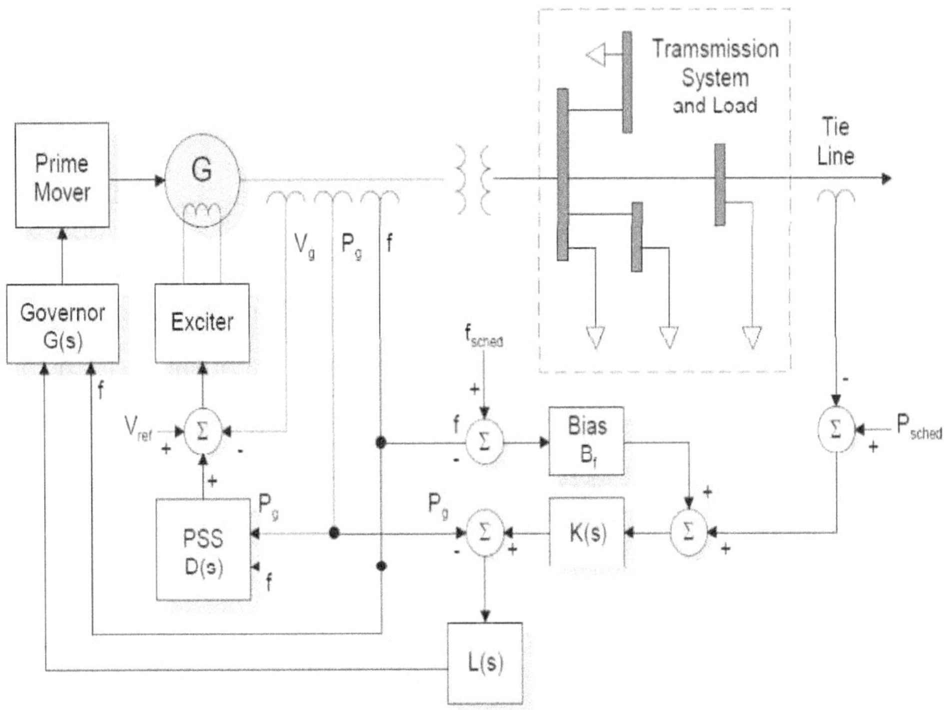

Figure 1.1 Control Schemes for a Generating Unit

Voltage Control Loop is to control the voltage at the terminals of the generator. It consists of the voltage regulator and exciter system. Inputs to this control loop are the reference voltage (V_{ref}), which may be chosen by the system dispatcher or automatically by computers (VAR dispatch) and the actual voltage at the terminals of the generator (V_g).

Power System Stabilizer (PSS) Loop is to slow down the oscillations of the generator subsequent to a disturbance. It comprises a feedback system which gives a stabilizing signal into the exciter system. Feedback quantities are frequency (f) and real power (P_g).

Primary Automatic Generator Control Loop is to control the real power output and the speed of the generator. It comprises the speed regulator (governor) of the prime mover. It utilizes feedback of the generator speed, frequency and the real power output of the generator.

Secondary Automatic Generation Control Loop is to control the net interchange, unit real power output and speed. It comprises a feedback system which provides a signal to the speed regulator (governor). The signal, known as the Unit Control Error (UCE) is generated from measurements of frequency, interchange schedule and unit real power output. Reference quantities for this control loop are: Scheduled interchange of real power (P_{shed}) and Scheduled frequency (f_{shed}). This control loop employs integral feedback of frequency and thus adjusts the system real time (integral of frequency).

As the electric power system is a dynamic system, the control loops should be designed in such a way that the system is steered to significant operating conditions and enhanced performance. It is clear that the controls connected with a generating unit are abundant and complex. Complexity is reduced with the operation of a hierarchical structure. For instance, at a higher level, the reference points for the generator control loops are determined such as interchange power (P_{shed}) and scheduled frequency (f_{shed}). At this level, economy and stability of the system are the principle considerations. Then, the above mentioned local control loops have the function of tracking the reference points. The higher level is carried out at a central location, the energy control centre. Based on the superiority of the particular energy management system, the reference points may be automatically chosen by computers or by operators.

For instance, the reference for the real power output of a unit may be automatically chosen by computers depending on a real time economic dispatch. Others, for instance, the frequency reference, may be chosen at another central location for a huge number of interconnected power systems depending on the divergence of the integral of the frequency from a correct time reference. All these conditions necessitate the continuous monitoring of the system conditions. This research mainly focuses on the power system stabilizer control loop Sakis Meliopoulos (1990).

This research aims at providing enhanced stability to the power system which in turn would enhance the overall performance of the system.

1.8 BASICS OF STABILITY

A mathematical model illustrating the functions of a power system comprises both differential and algebraic equations. A power system is generally subjected to continuous perturbations. For convenience, it is assumed that at a given operating level, the system is at rest, i.e., in equilibrium state. This in turn indicates that, a steady-state solution can be obtained to the equations illustrating the operation of the power system. Also, in order to be viable, the system states at the equilibrium must be within acceptable ranges.

Stability includes all kinds of stability likely to be encountered in power systems. The examples of different types of stability are synchronous stability, shaft torsional stability, voltage stability, control loop stability, etc. It is not essential to individually define voltage, or any other stability as most of the time they do not manifest themselves separately, i.e., they may be interrelated.

1.8.1 Power System Model and Its Stability

An interconnected power system basically consists of several essential components. They are the generating units, the transmission lines, the loads, the transformer, Static VAR (Volt Ampere Reactive) Compensators (SVC) and lastly the High Voltage Direct Current (HVDC) lines. During the operation of the generators, there may be some disturbances such as sustained oscillations in the speed or periodic variations in the torque that is applied to the generator.

These disturbances may result in voltage or frequency fluctuation that may affect the other parts of the interconnected power system. External factors, such as lightning, can also cause disturbances to the power system. All these disturbances are termed as faults. When a fault occurs, it causes the motor to lose synchronism if the natural frequency of oscillation coincides with the frequency of oscillation of the generators. With these factors in mind, the basic condition for a power system with stability is synchronism. Besides this condition, there are other important condition such as steady-state stability, transient stability, harmonics and disturbance, collapse of voltage and the loss of reactive power Khai Chiat Tham (2003).

The following conditions, although conservative in nature, can ensure cascading outages will not occur,

- When any of a specified set of disturbances occurs, the system will survive the ensuing transient and move into a steady-state condition.
- No bus voltage magnitudes during transients are outside their permissible ranges.

- In new steady-state condition, no control devices, equipment or transmission lines are overloaded and no bus voltage magnitudes are outside their permissible ranges (say 5% of nominal).

The first condition is related to the transient stability problem while the second one is related to the voltage-dip problem. These conditions are referred as dynamic stability. The third condition is referred as static stability by Hsiao-Dong Chiang et al. (1995).

1.8.1.1 Classification of stability

Figure 1.2 provides a comprehensive categorization of power system stability. There are two main classes of stability: angle stability and voltage stability. Angle stability has two main subclasses: small-signal (steady-state) stability and transient stability. A power system is considered to be steady-state stable if, after any small disturbance, it reaches a steady state operating condition which is identical or close to the pre disturbance operating condition. A power system is transient stable for a large disturbance or sequence of disturbances if, following that disturbance(s) it reaches an acceptable steady-state operating condition. Unlike steady-state stability which is a function only of the operating condition, transient stability is more complicated since it is a function of both operating condition and the disturbance. Voltage stability also has two main subclasses: large disturbance voltage stability and small-disturbance voltage stability.

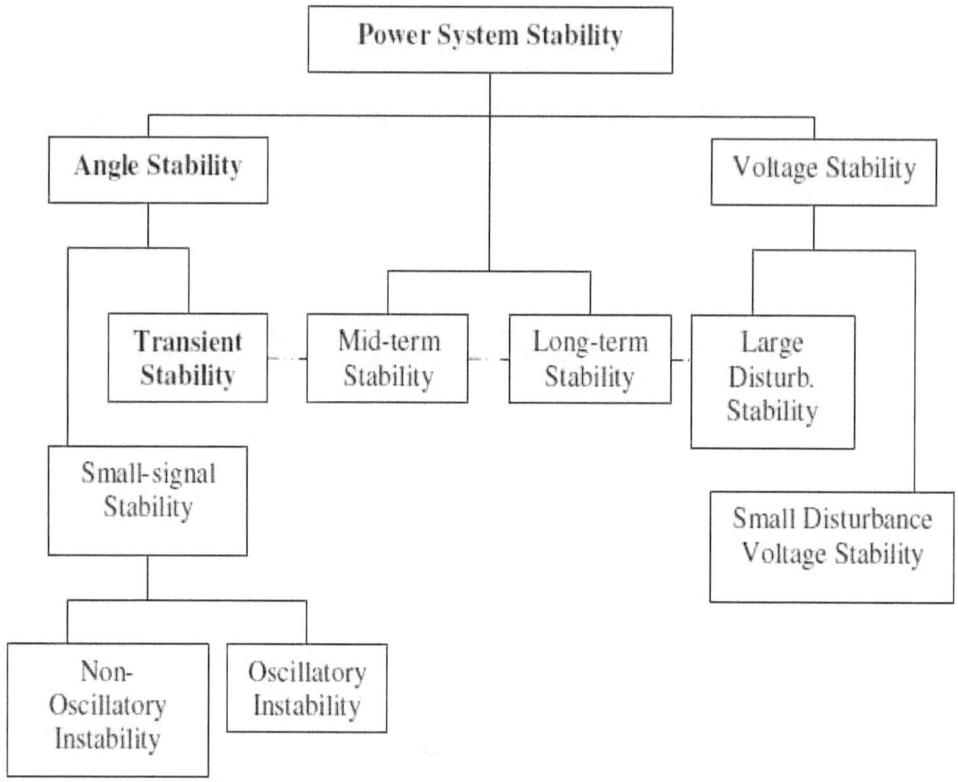

Figure 1.2 Classification of Power System Stability

For transient stability, it is usually when the power system experiences a large disturbance caused by an imbalance between the mechanical input and the electrical output powers. In order to study this type of stability, the focus is only on the first swing periodic drift. Therefore, only a fraction of a second is enough to observe the transients and several simulation time seconds to study the system. As of the small-signal stability, it occurs when the system lacks synchronizing torque or when an unstable control action occurs. This type of stability requires a study of more than a minute to several hours.

Small Signal Stability is the capacity of the power model to keep up synchronism when subjected to small disturbances Radhakrishna, (2010). Modern interconnected power systems are continuously growing in size and their stable operation is becoming more complex. Hence, the concept of stability of power systems has received a great deal of attention in recent years. Power system stability is the ability of an electrical power system to maintain synchronism, even when the system is subjected to various forms of disturbances and variations in operating conditions.

- The small-signal stability problem is usually one of insufficient damping of system oscillations.
- A disturbance is considered to be small if the conditions that portray the subsequent reaction of the structure might be linearized with the end goal of the investigation.

Rotor Angle Stability alludes to the capacity of a power structure to keep up synchronism when subjected to little and severe unsettling influences. The stability problem involves the study of electromechanical inertial oscillations experienced in power systems.

Voltage Stability is a major concern in planning and operations of power systems. It is well known that voltage instability and collapse have led to major system failures; with the development of power markets, more and more electric utilities are facing voltage stability-imposed limits as considered by Le Fu et al. (2008). The problem of voltage stability may be simply explained as inability of the power system to provide the reactive power or the egregious consumption of the reactive power by the system itself. Voltage stability is concerned with the ability of a power system to maintain required voltage profile at all buses in the system under steady state and also under transient state conditions.

The disadvantages of this practice are:

- It requires intensive time-consuming numerical integration; therefore it has not been suitable for on-line applications.
- It does not provide information regarding the degree of stability (when the system is stable) and the degree of instability (when the system is unstable).
- It does not provide information to derive preventive control when the system is deemed unstable.

It is often desirable in practice to perform many power system stability studies to examine the effects of different fault locations and types, various operating conditions, and different network topologies and control device characteristics. For a typical large power system, thousands of nonlinear differential and algebraic equations must be solved, which takes tens of minutes of Central Processing Unit (CPU) time on a modern computer. This intensive computation requirement imposes severe constraints on the number of cases which can be studied. Moreover, the current power system operating environment motivates moving transient stability assessment from the off-line planning area into the online operating environment. There are significant benefits expected from this movement.

First, one may be able to operate with margins reduced by a factor of 10 or more if the stability assessment is based on actual system configuration and operating conditions, instead of assumed worst case conditions, as is done in off-line studies. As a simple example, a power transfer corridor whose actual stability boundary on a given hour can be computed to be 2500 MW could be forced to operate at a limit of 2000 MW based on the conservative assumptions inherent to off-line analysis. An online stability assessment using the actual system topology and real-time data could compute a limit of 2450 MW with enough certainty to allow the operator to load the system to that point. The savings realized in increased MW transaction capability can be 10000 per hour. Another benefit of online analysis is that the amount of analysis can be reduced to those cases relevant to actual operating conditions. Thus, there is always considerable incentive to find superior calculation methods for stability analysis.

1.8.2 Stability Limits

Power systems should be designed to endure large disturbances and failures. Even certain power system apparatus are separated due to automatic protection and control actions, power supply to consumers will not be interrupted. Operational limits for the transmission network can be set through the following logic:

- The maximum power transmitted by each transmission line is restricted by its current carrying capacity, called as thermal limit.
- Any one of the lines, hitting the thermal limit, is utilized to attain the maximum loading of the transmission network. The loading of each line in the power system, variety of generator groups and load injections at the nodes at various operating conditions can create this limiting condition. Supervisory Control and Data Acquisition (SCADA) constantly ensures the thermal limit breaches as the operating condition alters over time.
- But, operating the system at a limiting state is not sensible as the loss of a transmission line or other equipment would probably overload some other lines.

- Therefore, the operating limit is not sensible when the first line hits its thermal limit but the loss of any one portion of apparatus will breaches thermal limit. This is called as the N-1 criterion for operation as any one of the N components of the power system can be lost without overloading any segment of the system.

- If a disturbance occurs, the first line of protection should separate the faulted apparatus. This is the rationality behind the N-1 criterion. It is the same disturbance which may cause instability determined. In such a scenario, the maximum loading of the system should be minimized which in turn restricts the instability. This loading limit is set by the stability criterion instead of the thermal loading. Stability limited power systems that are of interest in this research.

- If improved controls can enhance this stability limit, then the system can be loaded at a higher level. This offers better utilization of the transmission network.

The transmission limits are the conditions that also limit the power markets. Systems that are thermally restricted, the only technique to raise limits is to construct more transmission lines or systems. For those systems that are stability limited, better control techniques should be developed to increase the stability limit. Thus this research focuses on better control of stability in order to improve the performance of the power systems, Anjan Bose (2003).

1.9 POWER SYSTEM STABILIZER

Power system stability is one of the most important aspects in electric system operation. Due to increasing complexity of electric power systems, especially with the interconnection of these systems by weak tie lines, spontaneous system oscillations present limitations on power transfer capability and affect operational system economics and stability. Therefore, there is significant interest in the stabilization of such systems. By nature, a power system is continually experiencing disturbances. These may be classified as event disturbances and load disturbances.

Event disturbances include generator outages, short-circuits caused by lightning or other fault conditions, sudden large load changes, or a combination of such events. Event disturbances usually lead to a change in the configuration of the power system.

Load disturbances, on the other hand, are the small random fluctuations in load demands. The system configuration usually remains unchanged after load disturbances. Recent trends toward full utilization of existing generation and transmission systems have increased the effects of these disturbances on power system stability.

PSS is the most effective device to enhance the damping of electromechanical oscillations by providing supplementary stabilizing feedback signals in the excitation system. PSS augment the power system stability limit and extend the power transfer capability by enhancing the system damping of low-frequency oscillations in range of 0.2 to 2.5 Hz, Kundur (1994).

Numerous works are done and published around the world on the design of PSS for mitigating the effects of low-frequency oscillation mode. Among these, Conventional PSS (CPSS) of the lead-lag compensation type is used by most utility companies because of its simple structure, flexibility and ease of physical realization.

The CPSS is normally designed with a fixed gain, determined for a set of operating conditions. However, the nonlinear nature of the power system elements, wide range of operating conditions and unpredictable disturbances in the power system degrade the performance of such a fixed gain CPSS. To overcome the shortcomings of CPSS, many control strategies applying various techniques based on optimal control, robust control and adaptive control have been proposed and developed by the researchers around the world over the last three decades. Power System Stabilizers are attached to excitation systems to improve the damping of electric power system during low frequency oscillations.

1.10 MULTI-MACHINE POWER SYSTEM ANALYSIS

Investigations of practical power system includes the concurrent solution of equations governing synchronous machines, its related excitation system and prime movers, interconnecting transmission network, static and dynamic (motor) loads, other apparatus such as HVDC converters and static VAR compensators. The dynamics of the machine rotor circuits, excitation systems, prime mover and other devices are denoted by differential equations.

The outcome is that the entire system model comprises a large number of regular differential and algebraic equations.

The following assumptions are made for simplicity, Padiyar, (1996).

- The loads are denoted by constant impedances.
- Transient's saliency is eliminated by considering $x_q = x_{d'}$, where, $x_{d'}$ is d-axis transient reactance and x_q is q-axis synchronous reactance.
- Mechanical power is assumed to be constant.
- E_{tc} is single time constant Automatic Voltage Regulator (AVR).

Multi-Machine equations can be written similar to the one-machine system connected to the infinite bus. In order to reduce the complexity of the transient stability analysis, similar simplifying assumptions are made as follows:

- Each synchronous machine is represented by a constant voltage source behind the direct axis transient reactance. This representation neglects the effect of saliency and assumes constant flux linkages.
- The governor's action is neglected and the input powers are assumed to remain constant during the entire period of simulation.
- Using the pre-fault bus voltages, all loads are converted to equivalent admittances to ground and are assumed to remain constant.
- Damping or asynchronous powers are ignored.
- The mechanical rotor angle of each machine coincides with the angle of the voltage behind the machine reactance.

- Machines belonging to the same station swing together and are said to be coherent. A group of coherent machines is represented by one equivalent machine.

The first step in the transient stability analysis is to solve the initial load flow and to determine the initial bus voltage magnitudes and phase angles. The machine currents prior to disturbance are calculated in Equation (1.1), from the work of John et al. (1999).

$$I_i = \frac{S_i^*}{V_i^*} = \frac{P_i - jQ_i}{V_i^*}, 1 = 1, 2, \ldots, n \tag{1.1}$$

where n is the number of generators

S is the Stability level of the ith generator

V is the terminal voltage of the ith generator

P and Q are the real and reactive power of ith generator respectively.

All unknown values are determined from the initial power flow solution. The generator armature resistances are usually neglected and the voltages behind the transient reactance are then obtained as described by John et al. (1999) in Equation (1.2).

$$E_i^* = V_i + jX'_d I_i \tag{1.2}$$

E_i^* is the voltages behind the transient reactance

1.10.1 Synchronous Reactance or Steady State Condition Reactance

The synchronous reactance is the ratio of induced emf and the steady state rms current. It is the sum of leakage reactance (X_l) and the armature reactance (X_a) in Equation (1.3).

$$X_d = X_i + X_a \tag{1.3}$$

Transient reactance

The synchronous reactance is the ratio of induced emf on no load and the transient symmetrical rms current in Equation (1.4).

$$X'_d = X_1 + \frac{1}{\frac{1}{X_a} + \frac{1}{X_f}} \tag{1.4}$$

Next, all load are converted to equivalent admittances by using the relation in Equation (1.5).

$$y_{io} = \frac{S_i^*}{|V_i|^2} = \frac{P_i - jQ_i}{V_i^*} \tag{1.5}$$

1.11 MOTIVATION OF THE RESEARCH

Highly complicated power systems have been constructed to deal with the increasing demand. The development in electric power production is focused on the interconnected network of transmission lines linking generators and loads into huge integrated systems which helps in better supply of power. The characteristics of power system dynamic stability act as a field of research growing for ever because of the large scale interconnection of the power system. This field has been recognized as a significant problem for secure system operation from 1920's according to Soliman et al. (2008) and Bayliss & Hardy (2007) has put forth that there were various most important collapses resulted by the instability of a power system that indicates the significance of this trend. The maintenance of stability in a power system is considered as one of the highly important and necessary factors of power quality.

1.12 PROBLEM IDENTIFICATION

The highly complicated, dynamic activities and non-linearity of power systems along with their approximate continuous time variant nature have led to a great challenge to power system control engineers for several years. Classical PSS techniques do not guarantee the robustness of the system over a wide range of operating conditions. Classical stabilization approaches may represent adverse oscillations or lose of synchronism of the power system. Existing intelligent techniques for PSS exhibits poor global searching capability and convergence rate. Because of the drawbacks of the existing stabilization techniques, there is a need for a unique, simple, effective and economical approach for attaining stabilization of the power system.

The power system Stability estimation and power quality issues in grid systems have taken after issues.

- The difficulties in past measuring techniques are the necessity of equipment parts which makes them unacceptable and confused for the system based control system.
- The sensitivity of a structure to varieties of its parameters assumes a necessary part of investigation and monitoring
- Indeed, on the one hand, the estimations of model parameters vary from the notable ones (on account of errors in the figured information, of their variety with time, of defective acknowledgment of the controlled gadgets).
- On the other hand, data about the way the qualities of a structure rely on upon its parameter varieties might be utilized to enhance its exhibitions as, in versatile frames.

- It is vital to specify that lone static cut-off points are as of now used for both, blockage administration and controls. In any case, it concurs that all power system stability limits (static, voltage and transient) ought to be considered since the constraining condition in a few bits of the transmission systems can move among them after some time.
- Power system dynamic stability evaluation and control is presently an all the more requesting errand since, notwithstanding the common necessities of working force contexts, it has more imperatives, and new commitments and issues like the accompanying ones.
- Depending on the structure of the power showcase the old unit responsibility process is currently supplanted by a sale market that sets up the era profile for the next day or the following hour.
- The new capacity for making vitality contracts amongst clients and organizations for the long separation control transmission probably causes outsider wheeling. Keeping in mind the end goal to recognize and manage this clogging issue, it is in some cases essential that the framework administrator investigations bigger structures.
- This increments higher system many-sided quality is unsustainable for an independent gadget to balance out, and it will probably influence a client's trust.

1.13 RESEARCH CONTRIBUTION

Power System Stabilization methods have been suggested for a long period to improve the power system damping. The optimal sequential design for multi-machine power systems has become very essential and as a result, serious consideration is now being given on the concern of power system stabilization control. In recent times, the utilization of optimization techniques becomes possible to deal with control signals in power system.

As informed in the above area, to determine different issues distinguished in the wind plant, we have outlined different Stabilization strategies to enhance the execution of wind farm structures. We have planned three distinctive ways to deal with magnify the performance of force quality by considering several components. The point of the exploration is in Stabilize the power system with significant transient stability and to diminish the rotor instability with little aggregate consonant contortion by the accompanying systems.

1. **Rotor Angle Stability**-Stability Control of Doubly-Fed Induction Generator (DFIG) Using Genetic Heuristic (GH) Controller for Wind Farm

2. **Transient Stability**-Mitigation of Wind Farm Stabilization Using DFIG with DSTATCOM Compensation Scheme

1.14 OBJECTIVES

This work is meant to utilize quick and productive power system adjustment control using imaginative calculation which enhances the proficiency of force quality in high power applications.

- The explores primarily concentrate on the plan and advancement of superior controllers for Multimachine adjustment structure.

- The important goals of proposed system is to improve the power stability parameters in a multi-machine system.

- Modelling of Genetic Heuristic multi-machine controller with new optimization algorithm to attain the stability improvement in multi-machine power systems.
- Modelling of Hybrid coordinated controller with new optimization algorithm to reduce the settling time from faults conditions in Multimachine power systems.
- Modelling of Multimachine Power stability controller with enhanced optimization algorithm to attain the stability improvement in terms of maximum power overshoot in Multimachine power systems.

1.15 ORGANIZATION OF THE THESIS

The work manages a few Investigations on Power system adjustment for Wind plant system. The examination fundamentally concentrates on the plan and advancement of elite controllers for power system stabilizer. This research manages the change of power system adjustment utilizing several strategies to expand the power quality parameters and settle the system. The research work proposes different strategies for development of power system stabilizer and has created functional outcomes. The outcomes have been breaking down, and execution analysis is performed which results were gotten, and usage has been completed to guarantee the theory.

Chapter 1 discusses about the General presentation and inspiration for the proposed work and different power system stabilizer and plan systems to address the issue

Chapter 2 presents specific findings and review writing to complete the current work.

Chapter 3 clarifies about idea of Genetic Heuristic Controller (GHC) technique based wind modelling with PSS estimation and testing strategy.

Chapter 4 manages the Hybrid Coordinated Controller (HCC) based DFIG with DSTATCOM Compensation conspire for Power system stabilization.

Chapter 5 leads the Multimachine Power Stability Controller (MMPSC) of Power system change based power system stabilizer for the multi-machine system.

Chapter 6 examined the outcomes accomplished by before and proposed streamlining approach

Chapter 7 summarizes the commitments of the thesis by examination and difference of all the above methods for PSS and the future work are additionally included.

1.16 SUMMARY

This section gives the overall discussion about the basics of the power system. The transmission and the distribution nature of the power systems are also discussed in this chapter. The control functions employed in the power systems has been discussed in detail. The nature and the operation of the power system stabilizers and its importance have been thoroughly evaluated in this chapter. Moreover, this chapter deals with the application of optimization techniques in power system stabilization. A brief overview of the proposed approaches is also given in this chapter.

CHAPTER 2

LITERATURE SURVEY

2.1 INTRODUCTION

PSS tuning is a significant problem in electrical power system. Accurate parameters of PSS increase system stability margin. At the same time, tuning is a complicated task, as the power system being non-linear and its operating conditions vary. PSS tuning is the process of searching for the exact parameters that achieve acceptable performance for the power system. Basically tuning is based on the characteristics of generator system. The utilized CPSS are outlined using the hypothesis of stage remuneration in the recurrence area and are presented as a lead-slack compensator. The parameters of CPSS are resolved given the linearized model of the power system. Giving significant damping over a low working limit, the CPSS parameters ought to be pinched in light of the motions. Since power structures are exceedingly non-direct systems, with arrangements and working conditions modifying through time, the CPSS configuration because the linearized model of the power structure can't ensure its execution in a useful working environment. Subsequently, a versatile PSS which considers the non-direct nature of the plant and adjusts to the adjustments in the earth is required for the power system. With a particular end goal to enhance the execution of CPSSs, various strategies have been recommended for planning them, for example, smart advancement techniques Mahdiyeh Eslami et al. (2011) and Fuzzy Logic technique Taher and Shemshadi (2007). As of late fuzzy rationale based controller have been recommended for PSS outline. These are without display drivers where the correct mathematic model of the controlled system is not required. The control technique relies on an arrangement of tenets which depicts the conduct of the controller. The capacity to handle changes in working and system conditions and the ability of self-tuning of parameters to a particular degree are in-inherent such outline prepare Anup Singh and Indraneel Sen (2003). Likewise, numerous other distinctive strategies have been accounted for by Chatterjee et al. (2009), and the use of powerful control techniques for outlining PSS has been introduced by Gupta et al. (2005), Bouhamida et al. (2005) and Sil et al. (2009).

2.2 CONVENTIONAL TECHNIQUES AND THEIR DRAWBACKS ON FACTS CONTROLLER WITH PSS

As expressed before, the oscillation frequency area is between 0.5Hz to 3Hz. To expand the system damping, the phase lag of compensated system in this frequency zone ought not to be more than 90 degrees, Larsen, and Swann, (1981), which empowers the system to accomplish better execution. Thus, the stage remuneration ought to concentrate on the scope of 0.5Hz to 3Hz. For the frequency response of the structure without PSS (uncompensated system), modifies the period of the compensator by tuning the PSS parameters. At that point for the frequency response of the context with PSS (remunerated system) check if the stage slack is under 90 degree. If it doesn't meet the loose stage prerequisite, change the PSS parameters again and test the frequency reaction of the remunerated system again. By doing as such these two steps over and again, the system stage slack can be decreased mostly. Slack lead compensator based PSS are planned by the high-level pay. The significant disadvantages had of this strategy are the ascent time very long and it might at times result in the immersion of the PSS.

After all the PSS stage compensator parameters are settled, the root-locus of the remunerated system is plotted. From the root locus, the correct pickup esteem is chosen which doles out all roots to the open left half plane with the biggest conceivable damping proportion.

The other control strategy that can be utilized is a Proportional-Integral-Derivative (PID) controller whose coefficients are tuned in a versatile way with the system reaction stays in a conceived range Buamed and Shamekh (2002). The Proportional controller demonstrates a moderately high greatest overshoot, a long settling time and additionally a relentless state blunder. The Proportional-Integral (PI) controller intertwines the properties of the Proportional and Integral controllers. It demonstrates the greatest overshoot and settling time as the P controller, however, no unfaltering state mistake. The PID controller intertwines the properties of a PI and Proportional-Derivative (PD) controller. It demonstrates a littler most extreme overshoot than the PD controller and has no consistent state blunder because of the Integral activity.

The other option is to utilize shut circle tests. One approach is the established technique for Ziegler and Nichols (1942) which requires next to no data about the procedure. Notwithstanding, there are a few inconveniences. The Power system should be conveyed to its furthest reaches of shakiness, and various trials might be expected to carry the structure to this point. Another impediment is that the tunings don't function admirably on all procedures. It is outstanding that the suggested settings are very forceful for slack predominant (incorporating) forms and very moderate for overwhelming deferral process. A third detriment of the strategy is that it must be utilized in systems for which the stage slack surpasses 180° at high frequencies.

However, there are some strategies received for customary tuning of PSS, and the outline procedures are simply in light of the linearized model of the power system Reza Hemmati et al. (2010). It does not ensure the execution of PSS in a handy working environment. Subsequently, a versatile PSS which considers the non-straight nature of the plant and adjusts to the adjustments in the earth is required for the power system Liu et al. (2005). The utilization of versatile PSS as a controller for the power system is a strategy in which consideration has been paid as of late Chaturvedi and Malik, (2008) and FraileArdanuy and Zufiria (2007). The remarkable point about this PSS is that its coefficients are resolved utilizing creative consolidated strategies on various operational focuses.

Various research works as of now exist about the idea and difficulties in power quality system and power system strength, and some of them are assessed here.

The high infiltration of DFIG twist cultivates in power system may antagonistically affect on the damping of swaying modes because of the lessening of system inactivity, the collaboration among DFIG converter controls, the less synchronized coupling, and the uprooting of Synchronous Generators (SGs). These circumstances cause the confounded power motions issue which may prompt to wide range power outages. Under these situations, the CPSS will most likely be unable to handle the power moves.

To expand the PSS impact, the planned Power Oscillation Damper (POD) is altogether expected. As of late, the DFIG wind turbine which is furnished with the POD has been connected to stifle the power motions given the dynamic and responsive yield control of the DFIG. It makes the likelihood of the organized control of POD and PSS for the adjustment of force movements. In, the improved fractional Eigen-structure task for the outline of the consolidated PSS and POD is proposed. Moreover, the planned POD and PSS considering yield control variety is introduced.

The expected hearty control of the DFIG wind turbine and the PSS for adjustment of force motions considering system vulnerabilities is proposed in Adam Dysko et al. (2010). Think about outcomes demonstrate that the organized POD and PSS give preferred damping impact over the individual control of POD or PSS. Be that as it may, the POD and PSS in these works that utilization the nearby information signs may do not have the common perception of the between range modes. In like manner, the determination of appropriate info signs is profoundly required. To manage the between territory motions, the full region stability control is given synchronized Phasor Measurement Units (PMU) has been connected to the POD plan. In the vast area incorporated POD of the DFIG twist cultivate with pay for the correspondence dormancy is proposed.

Hansen Ghasemi (2006) explains wind energy can meet the growing energy needs of mankind due to its clean and inexhaustible nature. The Wind power generation has developed fast because of commercial application and large-scale development future. When the grid fault occurs, the stator flux would contain dc and negative sequence components which can induce large Electro Motive Force (EMF) in the rotor circuit. As a result, the generator rotor and the Rotor Side Converter (RSC) are prone to suffering from over currents if no additional protection measurement is employed.

Kayikci & Milanovic (2001) describes DFIG requires a crowbar protection system disconnects the converter in order to protect it, turning the DFIG generator into a squirrel cage induction generator. The crowbar may comprise of a set of thyristors that will short-circuit the rotor windings when triggered and thereby limit the rotor voltage and provide an additional path for the rotor current. Different values of the crowbar resistances result in a different behaviour.

Hu et al. (2002), describes the crowbar method works well even under severe grid faults; however, the controllability of DFIG is lost, and the electromagnetic torque of the DFIG oscillates greatly during the crowbar action, which will pose great press on the drive train. Moreover, the installation of extra hardware increases the cost and hinders its reliability.

Xiao et al. (2003), introduced a simple flux-linkage-tracking-based LVRT strategy is proposed for the control of RSC to suppress the fault rotor current. When the voltage dip is detected, the rotor flux linkage is controlled immediately to track a reduced fraction of the changing stator flux linkage by the control of RSC, and in this way, the rotor current can be effectively reduced. But this method is able to suppress rotor current effectively with much smaller torque oscillation.

Varadarajan & Swarp (2008), describes the problem of voltage instability can be solved by using dynamic reactive compensation. Shunt FACTS devices, such as the Static Var Compensator (SVC) and the Static Synchronous Compensator (STATCOM), have been widely used to provide high-performance steady state and transient voltage control at the Point of Common Coupling (PCC). The application of a STATCOM to help with the uninterrupted operation of a VSWT equipped with a DFIG during grid faults. The STATCOM is shunt connected at the bus where the wind turbine is connected to the power network to provide steady-state voltage regulation and improve the short-term transient voltage stability. But in some cases the complexity and additional cost impair their applicability.

Yuan & Fang (2009), analyzed the fundamental difficulty for the DFIG in ride-through is the EMF induced in the machine rotor during the fault, which depends on the dc and negative sequence components in the stator-flux linkage and the rotor speed. The investigation develops a control method to increase the probability of successful grid fault ride-through given the current and voltage capabilities of the rotor-side converter.

Almeida et al. (2004), describes about to control the active power and reactive power exchange between the machine and the grid, the rotor is fed by a link of AC-DC-AC converters modelled as voltage and controlled current sources, respectively. The control of the rotor-side converter is realized by fuzzy controllers whose performances are compared with that of conventional PI controllers.

Wang et al. (2008), describes about the alternative DFIG control targets during network unbalance, such as reducing stator current unbalance, torque, and power pulsations minimization, are identified. A rotor current control strategy based on positive and negative (dq) reference frames is used to provide precise control of the rotor positive and negative sequence currents.

Henceforth the proposition concentrates on creating strategies which essentially enhance the dependability examination with better proficiency and high power quality between systems with adequate postponement.

The most widely recognized challenges connected with established outline strategies are:

- Since control systems are exceedingly non-straight systems, with setups and parameters changing with time, the Conventional PSS configuration given a linearized model of the power system can't ensure its execution in every single working environment.

- In routine PSS the pickup settings are settled at specific qualities which are resolved just for a specific working condition.
- To give high damping over an extensive variety of working conditions, CPSS parameters should be calibrated because of all methods of motions present in the system.

Lately, fuzzy rationale based controller have been proposed for PSS plan. These are without display drivers. The correct mathematic model of the controlled system is not required. The control system relies on an arrangement of principles which portrays the conduct of the controller. The capacity to handle changes in working and system conditions and the capacity of self-tuning of parameters to a particular degree are in-implicit such outline prepare Anup Singh & Indraneel Sen (2003).

2.3 META-HEURISTICS: EVOLUTIONARY ALGORITHMS

Meta-heuristic algorithms are algorithms which, in order to escape from local optima, drive some basic heuristic: either a constructive heuristic starting from a null solution and adding elements to build a good complete one, or a local search heuristic starting from a complete solution and iteratively modifying some of its elements in order to achieve a better one Saad & Nada (2008). The meta-heuristic part permits the low level heuristic to obtain solutions better than those it could have achieved alone, even if iterated.

Evolutionary Algorithms (EA) are computer programs that attempt to solve complex problems by mimicking the processes of Darwinian evolution Darwin (1973). In an Evolutionary Algorithm a number of artificial creatures search over the space of the problem. They compete continually with each other to discover optimal areas of the search space. It is hoped that over time the most successful of these creatures will evolve to discover the optimal solution.

EA's consist of several heuristics, which are able to solve optimization tasks by imitating some aspects of natural evolution. They may use different levels of abstraction, but they are always working on whole populations of possible solutions for a given task. EA's are an approved set of heuristics, which are flexible to use and postulate only negligible requirements on the optimization task. The advantages of EA's are their adaptability to change and ability to quickly generate good enough solutions. EA's differ from other optimization methods in possessing the following features Ma & Lai (1995).

- The major property of EA heuristics is that the search space is not explored by starting with only one possible solution but with a whole population of possible solutions and that the individuals of the population can exchange solution attributes between them. This way EA heuristic can outperform a single or a Multi-Start Hill Climbing algorithm, since they are more resistant to premature convergence towards local optima in multimodal search spaces.

- EA methods are inherently quantitative; therefore they are well suited for parameter optimization. They can also be extended to multi-objective optimization. EA methods are easily combined with other optimization techniques by the use of memetic algorithms.

- EAs are payoff-driven. Payoffs may mean improvements in predictive power or return over a benchmark and such payoffs can predictive power or return over a benchmark and such payoffs can be easily translated to a fitness function for an EA. EA's, therefore, can deal with non-smooth, non-continuous, and non-differentiable functions that are the real-life optimization problems.

- EA methods allow a wide variety of extensions and constraints that EA methods allow a wide variety of extensions and constraints that cannot be provided in traditional methods. They are robust revealing a remarkable balance between efficiency and efficacy

- EAs use probabilistic transition rules, rather than deterministic rules, to select generations, so that they are a kind of stochastic optimization algorithm, which can search a complicated and uncertain area to find the global optimum. EAs are more flexible and robust than conventional optimization methods.

2.4 DIFFERENT METHODS OF EVOLUTIONARY ALGORITHMS

The most important categories of EA methods are Genetic Algorithms, Genetic Programming, Ant Colony Optimization (ACO), Evolutionary Strategies (ES) and Evolutionary Programming (EP).

2.4.1 Ant Colony Optimization

This method relies on achieving a balance between the exploration and exploitation. Thus, ACO algorithm is a new simulative evolutionary algorithm and was proposed in the year 1990s by the Italian scholar M. Dorigo. ACO is one of the techniques for global optimization inspired by the natural behaviour of social insects. More specifically, it takes its inspiration from the foraging behaviour of some ant species Marco Dorigo et al. (2006). ACO is also a paradigm for designing meta-heuristic algorithms for combinatorial optimization problems. The essential trait of ACO algorithms is the combination of a priori information about the structure of a promising solution with posterior information about the structure of previously obtained good solutions. The main idea of ACO is to model a problem as the search for a minimum cost path in a graph. Artificial ants walk on this graph as if looking for cheaper paths. Each ant has a rather simple behaviour capable of finding relatively costlier paths. Cheaper paths are found as the emergent result of the global cooperation among ants in the colony. The behaviour of artificial ants is inspired from real ants: they lay pheromone trails (obviously in a mathematical form) on the graph edges and choose their path with respect to probabilities that depend on pheromone trails. These pheromone trails progressively decrease by evaporation. In addition, artificial ants have some extra features not seen in their counterpart in real ants. In particular, they live in a discrete world (a graph) and their moves consist of transitions from nodes to nodes Selvi & Umarani (2010).

The ACO differs from the classical ant system in the sense that here the pheromone trails are updated in two ways. Firstly, when ants construct a tour they locally change the amount of pheromone on the visited edges by a local updating role. Secondly, after all the ants have built their individual tours, a global updating rule is applied to modify the pheromone level on the edges that belong to the best ant tour found so far.

A parametric probabilistic model is a set of probability distributions indexed by a finite-dimensional parameter vector. In the problem selected, ACO algorithm is based on a parameterized probabilistic model where the pheromone model is used to model the chemical pheromone trails and a probabilistic technique for solving computational problems which can be reduced to finding good paths through graphs. The pheromone-based parameterized probabilistic model for the ACO algorithm is presented as the construction graph that the combinatorial optimization problem can be mapped on. Based on the construction graph, the solution construction procedure and update rule of pheromone model in the ACO algorithm can be illustrated Xiao-Rong Wang (2003).

The ACO has the following features:

- ACO uses a parameterized probabilistic model to construct solutions that are then used to update the model parameter values with the aim of increasing the probability of constructing high quality solutions Deng feng Xu & Liping Fu (2009).

- Inherent parallelism.

- Positive Feedback accounts for rapid discovery of good solutions.

- Efficient for Travelling Salesman Problem and similar problems.

- Can be used in dynamic applications.

- This proposed meta-heuristic approach is used for solving hard combinatorial optimization problems.

2.4.2 Genetic Algorithm

Genetic algorithm is an optimization algorithm based on the mechanics of natural selection and genetics. In GA, candidate solutions to the given problem are analogous to individuals in a population. Each individual is encoded as a string, called chromosome. New candidate solutions are produced from parent chromosomes by the crossover operator. The mutation operator is then applied to the population. The quality of each individual is evaluated and rated by the so called fitness function. Similar to the natural selection mechanism in the biological system, the fitter individuals have more chance to pass on information to the next generation. When a chromosome with the desired fitness is obtained, it will be taken as the optimal solution, and the optimization process is terminated. Otherwise, the process is repeated until the maximum number of generations is reached and the fittest chromosome so far obtained is taken to be the optimal solution.

GA has the following features:

- GA searches from a population of points, not based on single point. GA does not require linearity, continuity, or differentiability of the objective function, nor do they need continuous variables.
- Treats integer and discrete variables naturally.
- GA has inherent parallel computation ability.
- GA can quickly scan a vast solution set. Bad proposals do not affect the end solution negatively as they are simply

discarded. The inductive nature of the GA means that it doesn't have to know any rules of the problem instead it works by its own internal rules. This is very useful for complex or loosely defined problems.

2.4.3 Differential Evolution

A classical overview of Differential Evolution (DE) and terse introduction to the approach for function optimization has been presented by Storn & Price (1997). DE is a population-based, stochastic function optimizer using vector differences for perturbing the population. DE often exhibits a compelling performance advantage over conventional genetic algorithms. Differential evolution is a simple population based, stochastic parallel search evolutionary algorithm for global optimization and solves real valued problems based on the principles of natural evolution.

DE is capable of handling non-differentiable, non-linear, and multi- modal objective functions. In DE, the population consists of real valued vectors which equal the number of design parameters/control variables. The population of a DE algorithm is randomly initialized within the initial parameter bounds. The optimization process is conducted by means of three main operations: mutation, crossover and selection. In each generation, each individual of the current population becomes a target vector. For each target vector, the mutation operation produces a mutant vector, by adding the weighted difference between two randomly chosen vectors to a third vector. The crossover operation generates a new vector, called trial vector, by mixing the parameters of the mutant vector with those of the target vector. If the trial vector obtains a better fitness value than the target vector, then the trial vector replaces the target vector in the next generation Varadharajan & Swarup (2008). The features of DE are given below:

This approach utilizes already computed pieces of information and does not require extra function evaluations.

- This method potentially, alleviates problems such as the decreased rate of convergence, divergence and premature saturation.
- Extracting distance and direction information from the population to generate random deviations result in an adaptive scheme with excellent convergence properties.
- DE is generally more efficient and robust with respect to reproducing close results in different runs Zhen zhi Lin et al. (2008).
- DE is simple to implement and needs little tuning on its parameters.
- DE differs from other EA in the mutation and recombination process. Unlike stochastic techniques such as GA and Evolutionary Strategies, where perturbation occurs in accordance with a random quantity, DE uses weighted differences between solution vectors to perturb the population.
- DE employs a greedy selection process with implicit elitist features.
- DE algorithm is able to find the optimal solution for the functions with less number of generations and outcomes with better performance than other algorithms.

2.5 SUMMARY

In this chapter, the applications of conventional techniques for tuning PSS along with their drawbacks are discussed. The FACTS technique is also discussed. The suitability of the evolutionary algorithms such as PCO, GA and DE to design PSS are presented.

CHAPTER 3

MODELING OF GENETIC HEURISTIC CONTROL FOR WIND ENERGY BASED POWER SYSTEM STABILIZER

3.1 INTRODUCTION

The main aim of this chapter is to present a clear description and mathematical modelling of the different modules in a DFIG based wind generation system. Before discussing mathematical modelling, the basic concepts of a wind energy generation system, when connected to a utility grid, are presented to ensure a clear understanding of its characteristics and operations. It provides a detailed description of the classification of grid integrated wind energy generation systems, and then presents the importance of the system as well as the factors that lead to the choice of a DFIG as the generator for this thesis. It will offer a literature review of DFIGs and conventional controllers. The mathematical modelling background of all the modules of DFIG based wind generation systems is presented. Finally, the chapter ends with a summary describing the importance of chapter 3.

3.2 WIND ENERGY CONVERSION SYSTEM

Rising pollution levels and worrying changes in climate, arising in great part from energy producing processes, demand the reduction of ever-increasing environmentally damaging emissions discussed in Abbas et al. (2001). Additionally an emerging awareness of finiteness of the earth's fossil fuel reserves has caused many people to look for alternatives. Generating electricity, particularly by making use of renewable resources, allows the attainment of notable effects. A number of renewable power generation sources exist, such as wind energy, solar energy, wave energy, hydro-power and more sophisticated systems based on Hydrogen. In renewable power generation, wind energy has been noted as the most rapidly growing technology; it attracts interests as one of the most cost-effective ways to generate electricity from renewable sources.

Wind power generation has urbanized fast because of large-scale industrial application and commercial applications in future. In the wind energy conversion system consists of AC generator or DC generator. The generators are used to convert mechanical power of a wind turbine is converted into electric power. The most widely used synchronous machine or an induction machine as an AC generator in the wind power industry. The electromagnetic principle of action and reaction flux are produced in electrical machine. The same machine can be used as a motor for converting electric power into mechanical power or as a generator for converting mechanical power into electric power.

The conventional DC machine is either self-excited by shunt or by series coils carrying DC current to produce a magnetic field. The modern DC machine is often designed with permanent magnets to eliminate the field current requirement, hence, the commutator. The permanent-magnet DC machine is used with small wind turbines. However, due to limitations of the permanent-magnet capacity and strength, the brushless DC machine is generally limited to ratings below 100 kW.

The synchronous machine, when used in a grid-connected system, has some advantages over the induction machine. It does not require reactive power from the grid. The synchronous generator is rarely used in gear-driven wind systems. However, the low-speed design of the synchronous generator is often found advantageous in the direct-drive variable-speed wind turbine. In such a design, the generator is completely decoupled from the grid by a voltage source power electronic converter connected to the stator, and the rotor is excited by an excitation winding or a permanent magnet.

The DFIG is currently the system of choice for multi-MW wind turbines. Variable speed induction generators and particularly DFIGs are more and more used for wind energy conversion. The DFIG system operates in both sub- and super-synchronous modes with a rotor speed range around the synchronous speed. The stator circuit is directly connected to the grid while the rotor winding is connected via slip-rings to a three-phase converter. If the machine is producing torque and operating as a motor, the rotor will generate power if the speed is below synchronous speed (sub-synchronous operation). At standstill all active power fed in the stator (excluding losses) is returned via the rotor. If the machine is operating as a motor at speeds over the synchronous speed (super-synchronous operation), the mechanical power is fed in both through the stator and rotor.

3.3 STRUCTURE OF DFIG

DFIG is generating principle widely used in wind turbines as shown in Figure 3.1. It is based on an induction generator with a multiphase wound rotor and a multiphase slip ring assembly with brushes for access to the rotor windings. It is possible to avoid the multiphase slip ring assembly (see brushless doubly fed electric machines), but there are problems with efficiency, cost and size. A better alternative is a brushless wound-rotor doubly fed electric machine.

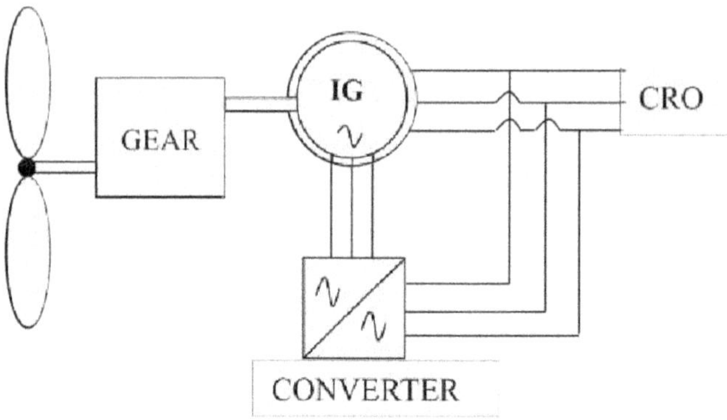

Figure 3.1 Principle of a Doubly Fed Induction Generator connected to a wind turbine

The principle of the DFIG is that rotor windings are connected to the grid via slip rings and back-to-back voltage source converter that controls both the rotor and the grid currents. Thus rotor frequency can freely differ from the grid frequency (50 or 60 Hz). By using the converter to control the rotor currents, it is possible to adjust the active and reactive power fed to the grid from the stator independently of the generator's turning speed. The control principle used is either the two-axis current vector control or Direct Torque Control (DTC). DTC has turned out to have better stability than current vector control especially when high reactive currents are required from the generator.

The DFIG rotors are typically wound with 2 to 3 times the number of turns of the stator. This means that the rotor voltages will be higher and currents respectively lower. Thus in the typical ± 30% operational speed range around the synchronous speed, the rated current of the converter is accordingly lower which leads to a lower cost of the converter.

3.4 DFIG WITH CROWBAR ARRANGEMENT

The crowbar arrangement based protection system is used to avoid the faults in the doubly fed induction wind generators discussed by Abdel-Maid et al. (1999) and (2003). The insertion of the crowbar in the rotor circuits for a short period of time control the terminal voltage values. The crowbar consists of resistors, which are controlled by power electronic devices as shown in Figure 3.2.

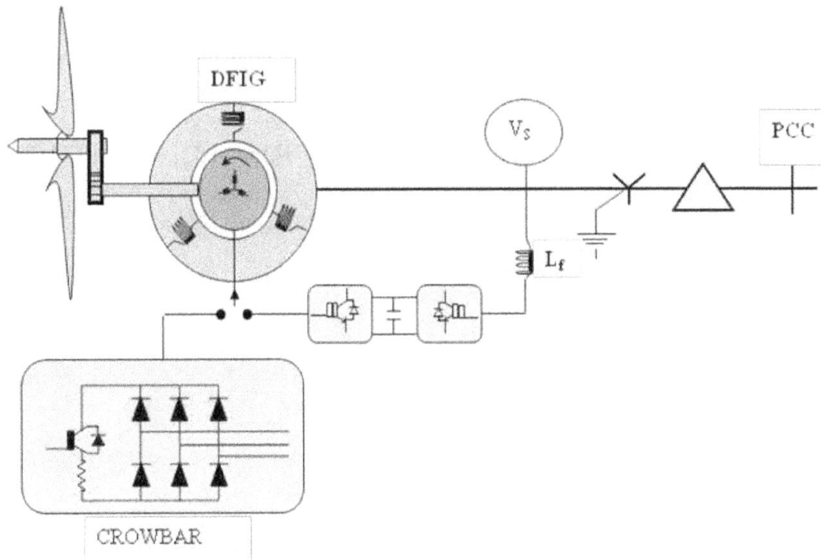

Figure 3.2 DFIG protected by the crowbar arrangement

With this solution, the machine is effectively protected, but due to the fact that the blocking of the rotor-side converter leads to the partial loss of power control during the crowbar action, large transients are generated after the fault, which may lead to the disconnection of the machines from the grid Abido & Abdel – Magid (2002). In addition, during the activation of the crowbar, the DFIG is converted to a conventional squirrel-cage induction generator, absorbing a large amount of reactive power from the grid.

However, the controllability of DFIG is lost, and the electromagnetic torque of the DFIG oscillates greatly during the crowbar action, which will pose great press on the drive train. Moreover, the installation of extra hardware increases the cost and hinders its reliability. Although an active crowbar is able to protect the RSC, it simultaneously changes a DFIG into a conventional squirrel cage induction generator, which absorbs a large amount of reactive power from the power grid and they cannot generate reactive power during the activation of the crowbar Abido & Abdel – Magid (1998) and (1999). With this behaviour, the grid voltage dip is further deteriorated.

3.5 DFIG USING GENETIC HEURISTIC CONTROLLER (GHC)

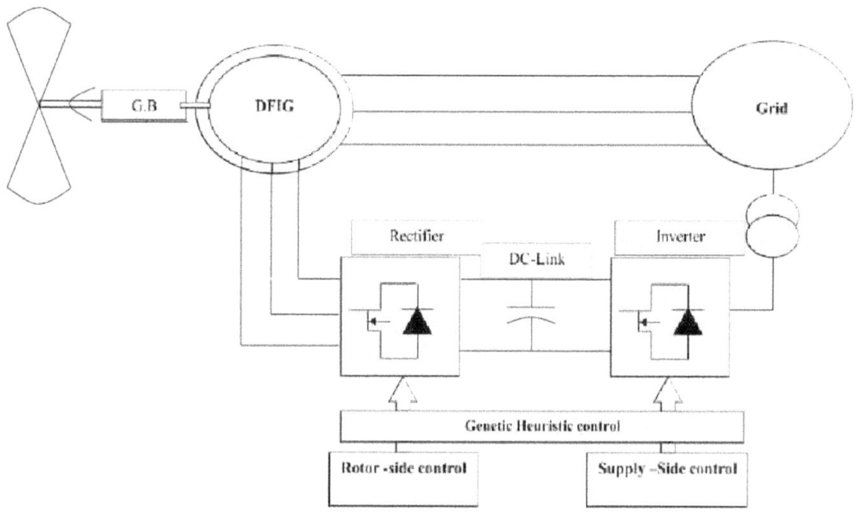

Figure 3.3 DFIG without crowbar arrangement

In this proposed method, a new computational intelligence-based control strategy, to enhance the low voltage ride-through capability of grid-connected WTs with DFIGs. A planned control technique to enhance the LVRT ability of lattice associated DFIG WTs without the need of any assistant equipment. The coordinated control among the RSC converter and Grid Side Converter (GSC) presented in Abido (2001). Figure 3.3 shows the DFIG without crowbar arrangement.

Compared with the crowbar method, the faults can be ride-through without any additional hardware, and the DFIG is still under control during the faults, which improves the controllability of the whole system Abido (2002). Therefore, instead of firing crowbar, it is more desirable to ride-through the faults by the proper control of RSC.

3.6 BLOCK DIAGRAM

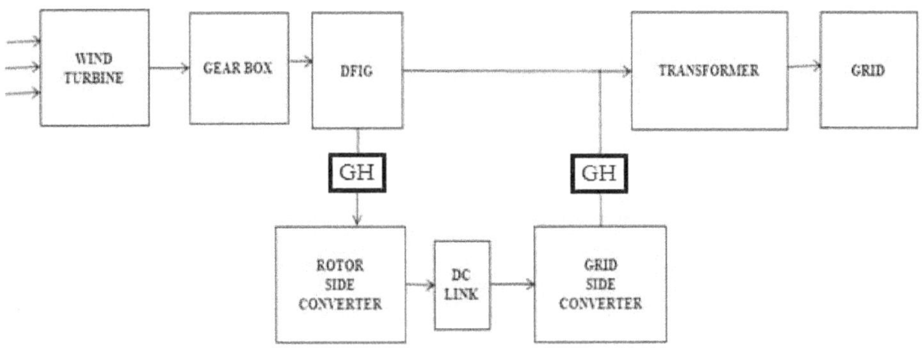

Figure 3.4 Block diagram of the DFIG Wind Turbine

The proposed design flow is shown in Figure 3.4. It has various components in the proposed system are as follows.

3.7 COMPONENTS DESCRIPTION

3.7.1 Wind Turbine

Wind turbines tend to be type-certified for clearly defined external conditions. This certification is requested by investors and insurance companies, and states that wind turbines will be secure and fit for their purpose for their intended lifetime of around 20 years for onshore projects and 25 years for offshore.

The costs of wind turbine installation include notably:

- Foundations
- Road construction
- Underground cabling within the wind farm
- Low to medium voltage transformers
- Medium to high voltage substation (sometimes)
- Transport, craning
- Assembly and test
- Administrative, financing and legal costs

3.7.1.1 Electrical grid connection

Large wind farms are generally connected to the high voltage electrical transmission grid (usually 60 kV and above), whereas individual wind turbines or clusters of turbines are generally connected to the distribution grid (8-30 kV). If the local grid is already saturated with other electrical equipment, there may be the additional costs of upgrading the grid to accommodate the wind turbines.

3.7.1.2 Gear box

Gear box needed to increase speed to 1200-1800 RPM for generator. With engine rotation and the clutch engaged, the input shaft transfers its motion through the counter-shaft, to rotate the gears on the main shaft. In this neutral condition, the engagement sleeves and hubs splinted to the output shaft are stationary. No drive is transmitted to the output.

Depressing the clutch pedal removes the engine load from the input. This allows an engagement sleeve to be moved into engagement with the external teeth on the gear selected. This locks the gear to the main shaft. When the clutch is released, the drive is transmitted to the input gears, along the counter-shaft to the gear selected. Since this gear is now locked to the main shaft, the main shaft rotates and transfers the drive to the final drive unit. The speed ratio and the torque transferred depend on which gear is selected. Twisting power from the engine hits the gearbox via the clutch and spins the countershaft.

3.7.2 Power Converters

This section will detail the AC-DC-AC converter used on the rotor which consists of two voltage-sourced converters, i.e., RSC and GSC, which are connected "back-to-back" Anup singh & Indraneel Sen (2003) and Bayne et al. (1977). Between the two converters a dc-link capacitor is placed, as energy storage, in order to keep the voltage variations (or ripple) in the dc-link voltage small. With the RSC it is possible to control the torque or the speed of the DFIG and also the power factor at the stator terminals, while the main objective for the grid-side converter is to keep the dc-link voltage constant regardless of the magnitude and direction of the rotor power Adam dysko et al. (2010). The grid-side converter works at the grid frequency (leading or lagging in order to generate or absorb a controllable magnitude of reactive power). A transformer may be connected between the grid-side inverter or the stator, and the grid. The rotor-side converter works at different frequencies, depending on the wind speed.

The back-to-back arrangement of the converters provides a mechanism of converting the variable voltage, variable frequency output of the generator (as its speed changes) into a fixed frequency, fixed voltage output compliant with the grid. The DC link capacitance is an energy storage element that provides the energy buffer required between the generator and the grid.

3.7.2.1 Rotor side converter

A rectifier is a circuit that converts an AC signal into a unidirectional signal. It is a type of DC-AC converter. A three-phase bridge rectifier is commonly used in high power applications. It can operate with or without a transformer and gives six-pulse ripples on the output voltage. The switches are numbered in order of conduction sequences and each one conducts for 120°. The pair of switches which are connected between that pair of supply lines having the highest amount of instantaneous line-to-line voltage will conduct.

RSC is used to control the torque production of the DFIG through direct control of the rotor currents Arumugam Jeevanandham & Keppana (2009) and Buamed & Shamekh (2002). The RSC does this by applying a voltage to the rotor windings that corresponds to the desired current. The RSC will operate at varying frequencies corresponding to the variable rotor speed requirements based on the wind speed. The RSC can use either a torque controller, speed controller, or active power controller to regulate the output power of the DFIG. This output power is controlled to follow the wind turbine's power-speed characteristic curve. Essentially, any given wind speed corresponds to an amount of available power that can be extracted from the wind. In order to extract this power most efficiently, the optimal tip-speed ratio must be kept before rated power is reached, corresponding to a different rotor speed for each power level. This calculation is done for any given wind turbine, resulting in a unique power-speed characteristic curve.

The actual output power from the generator, plus all power losses, is compared to this reference power from the power-speed curve. Typically a PI controller is used to control the torque, speed, or power to its reference value Buamed & Shamekh (2002). Whichever controller is used, the output of the controller is the reference rotor current required to generate the desired torque or power, or to obtain the desired speed. An inner PI control loop is then used to control the rotor current error to its reference value, with the rotor voltage reference as the controller output. The rotor current can also be used to control the reactive power production of the DFIG. The details of both the torque and reactive power control will be elucidated in the section Control of the DFIG Machine.

3.7.2.2 Grid side converter

The GSC is used to regulate the voltage of the DC link between the two converters as shown in Figure 3.5. The GSC contains on outer loop control that controls the DC-link voltage, attempting to control it to nominal value. An inner PI control loop controls the GSC current. Commonly the GSC acts to set Qgc = 0 and maximize active power output. As the GSC is connected directly to the grid, it must output power at a fixed frequency corresponding to the grid frequency.

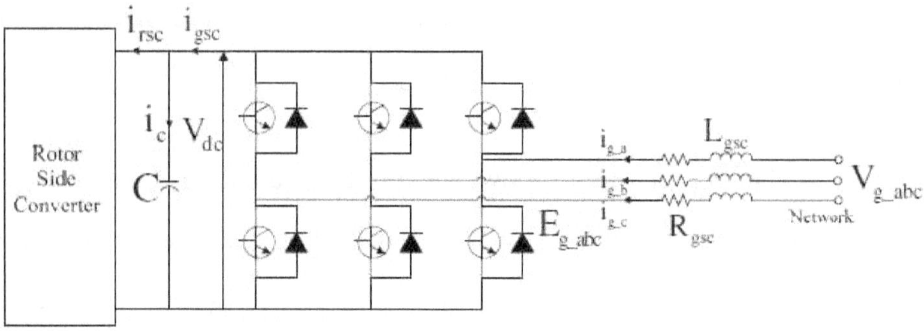

Figure 3.5 Grid-Side Converter Configuration

DC-to-AC converters are known as inverters. The function of an inverter is to change a DC input voltage to a symmetric AC output voltage of desired magnitude and frequency. The output voltage could be fixed or variable at a fixed or variable frequency. A variable output voltage can be obtained by varying the input DC voltage and maintaining the gain of the inverter constant. The inverter gain may be defined as the ratio of the AC output voltage to the DC input voltage.

3.8 DFIG WIND TURBINE SYSTEM MODEL

The wind turbine model studied in this research is illustrated. In this system, the wind turbine is connected to the DFIG through a drive train system, which consist of a low and a high speed shaft with a gearbox in between Anderson and Fouad (1977), and Anup Singh and Indraneel (2003). The DFIG system is an induction type generator in which the stator windings are directly connected to the three-phase grid and the rotor windings are fed through three-phase back-to-back IGBT based PWM converters. The back-to-back PWM converter consist of three parts a RSC, a GSC and a dc link capacitor placed between the two converters. There controller also consists of three parts RSC, GSC and wind turbine controller. The function of these controllers are to produce smooth electrical power with constant voltage and frequency to the power grid whenever the wind system is working at sub-synchronous speed or super-synchronous speed, depending on the velocity of the wind. Vector control strategy is employed for both the RSC and GSC to achieve decoupled control of active and reactive power.

3.8.1 Model of Generator

The operating principle of a DFIG can be analyzed using the classic theory of rotating fields and the well-known d-q model as shown in Figure 3.6, as well as both three-to-two and two-to-three axes transformations. In order to deal with the machine dynamic behaviour in the most realistic possible way, both stator and rotor variables are referred to their corresponding natural reference frames in the developed model.

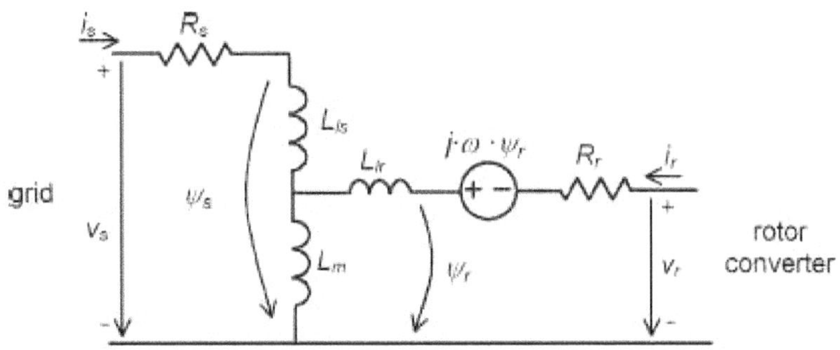

Figure 3.6 Equivalent DFIG model

The DFIG voltage and flux equations, expressed in Park reference frame, are given by Equations (3.1) and (3.2).

$$v_{ds} = -R_s i_{ds} - \omega_s \lambda_{qs} + \frac{d\lambda}{d\tau}\frac{d\lambda}{d\tau}{}^{qs} \tag{3.1}$$

$$v_{qs} = -R_s i_{qs} + \omega_s \lambda_{ds} + \frac{d\lambda}{d\tau}\frac{d\lambda}{d\tau}^{qs} \tag{3.2}$$

$$v_{dr} = R_r I_{dr} - (\omega_s - \omega_r)\,\lambda_{qr} + \frac{d\lambda}{d\tau}\frac{d\lambda}{d\tau}^{dr}$$

(3.3)

$$v_{qr} = R_r i_{qr} + (\omega_s - \omega_r)\,\lambda_{dr} + \frac{d\lambda}{d\tau}\frac{d\lambda}{d\tau}^{qr}$$

(3.4)

The indices d and q indicate the direct and quadrature axis components of the reference frame.

The flux linkage in Equations (3.3) and (3.4) is defined as Equations (3.5) to (3.8).

$$\lambda_{ds} = -L_s\, i_{ds} + L_m i_{dr} \tag{3.5}$$

$$\lambda_{qs} = -L_s i_{qs} + L_m i_{qr} \tag{3.6}$$

$$\lambda_{dr} = L_r i_{dr} + L_m\, i_{ds} \tag{3.7}$$

$$\lambda_{qr} = L_r i_{qr} + L_m i_{qs} \tag{3.8}$$

In other words, the stator side current and voltage components are referred to a stationary reference frame, while the rotor side current and voltage components are referred to a reference frame rotating at rotor electrical speed.

3.8.2 Model of Drive Train

The drive train system consists of turbine, a low and a high speed shaft, and a gearbox. This system can be represented by a two-mass model as follows Equations (3.9) to (3.12).

$$2\,H_t \frac{d\omega}{d\tau} = T_m - T_{sh} \tag{3.9}$$

$$\frac{d\theta t\omega}{d\tau} = \omega_t - \omega_r = \omega_t - (1-S_r)\,\omega_s \tag{3.10}$$

$$2H_g \frac{ds\gamma}{d\tau} = -T_{em} - T_{sh} \tag{3.11}$$

$$T_{sh} = K_{sh}\Theta_{t\omega} + D_{sh}\frac{d\theta\tau\omega}{d\tau} \tag{3.12}$$

Where

H_t the inertia constants of the turbine

H_g the inertia constants of the generator

ω_t the WT angle speed

ω_r the generator rotor angle speed

$\Theta_{t\omega}$ the shaft twist angle

K_{sh} the shaft stiffness coefficient

$D_{sh}$the damping coefficient

T_{sh} the shaft torque

T_m the wind torque

$T_{em}$the electromagnetic torque

T_m and T_{em} are given by Equations (3.13) to (3.15).

$$T_m = \frac{0.5\rho\pi R2CpV\omega 3}{\omega\tau} \tag{3.13}$$

$$T_{em} = \frac{Ps}{\omega\tau} \tag{3.14}$$

$$C_p = \frac{1}{2} \frac{Rcf}{(\lambda - 0.022\beta - 2)} e^{-0.225Rcf/\lambda} \tag{3.15}$$

ρ the air density

R the WT blade radius

V_ω the wind speed

C_f the blade design constant coefficient

β the blade pitch angle

λ the blade tip speed ratio

ω_s the synchronous angle speed

C_p the power coefficient

P_s the stator active power

3.8.3 Model of DC Link Capacitor

From the active power flow through the back-to-back PWM converter is balanced by the dc link capacitor. The power balance equation can be represented as follow,

$$P_r = P_g + P_{DC} \tag{3.16}$$

where

P_r the active power at the ac terminal of the RSC

P_g the active power at the ac terminal of the GSC

P_{DC} the active power of the dc link capacitor

These are given by following equations

$$P_r = v_{dr}i_{dr} + v_{qr}i_{qr} \tag{3.17}$$

$$P_g = v_{dg}i_{dg} + v_{qg}i_{qg} \tag{3.18}$$

$$P_{DC} = v_{DC}i_{DC} = -Cv_{DC}\frac{dvDC}{d\tau} \tag{3.19}$$

where

i_{dr} the axis rotor currents

i_{qr} the axis rotor currents

i_{dg} the axis currents of the GSC

i_{qg} the axis currents of the GSC

v_{dr} the axis rotor voltage

v_{qr} the axis rotor voltage

v_{dg} the axis voltage of the GSC

v_{qg} the axis voltage of the GSC

v_{DC} the dc link capacitor voltage

i_{DC} the current of the dc link capacitor

C the capacitance of the dc link capacitor

Substituting Equations (3.17) to (3.19) into Equation (3.16), the model of the dc link capacitor can be derived as follows Equation (3.20).

$$C\, v_{DC} \frac{dv_{DC}}{d\tau} = v_{dg} i_{dg} + v_{qg} i_{qg} - (v_{dr} i_{dr} + v_{qr} i_{qr}) \tag{3.20}$$

3.8.4 Model of Rotor Side Controller

As mentioned earlier, the vector control strategy is used for the active power and reactive power control of WT with DFIG system. For the RSC controller, the active power and voltage are controlled independently via v_{qr} and v_{dr}, respectively. The schematic diagram of rotor side controller is shown in Figure 3.7.

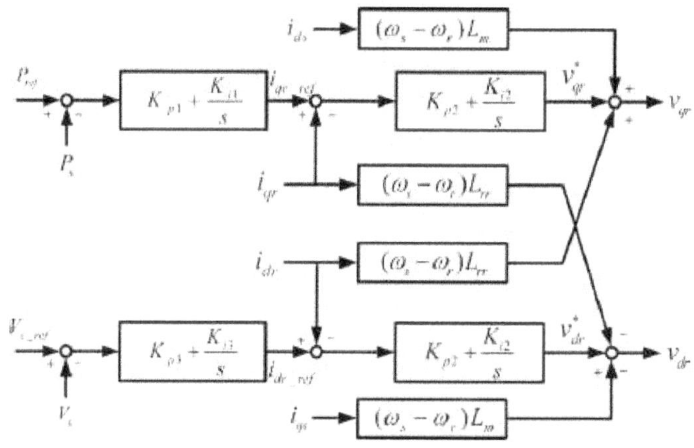

Figure 3.7 Schematic diagram of rotor side controller

While control equations can be expressed as follow the Equations 3.21 to 3.28.

$$\frac{dx1}{d\tau} = P_{ref} + P_s \tag{3.21}$$

$$i_{qr\_ref} = K(P_{ref} + P_s) + K_{i1}\, x_1 \tag{3.22}$$

$$\frac{dx2}{d\tau} = i_{qr\_ref} - i_{qr} = K_{p1}\ (P_{ref}+P_s) + K_{i1}\ x_1\text{-}i_{qr} \quad (3.23)$$

$$\frac{dx3}{d\tau} = v_{s\_ref} - v_s \quad (3.24)$$

$$i_{dr\_ref} = K_{p3}(v_{s\_ref} - v_s) + K_{i3}x_3 \quad (3.25)$$

$$\frac{dx4}{d\tau} = i_{dr\_ref} - i_{dr} = K_{p3}(v_{s\_ref}\text{-}v_s) + K_{i3}x_3 - i_{dr} \quad (3.26)$$

$$v_{qr} = K_{p2}\ (K_{p1}\Delta P + K_{i1}\ x_1\text{-}i_{qr}) + K_{i2}\ x_2 + S_r\omega_s L_m i_{ds} + S_r\omega_s L_{rr} i_{qr} \quad (3.27)$$

$$v_{dr} = K_{p2}(K_{p3}\Delta v + K_{i3}\ x_3\text{-}i_{dr}) + K_{i2}\ x_4\ - S_r\omega_s L_m i_{qs}\ - S_r\omega_s L_{rr} i_{dr} \quad (3.28)$$

Where

K_{p1} & K_{i1} the PI gains of the power regulator

K_{p2} & K_{i2} the PI gains of RSC current regulator

K_{p3} & K_{i3} the PI gains of the grid voltage regulator

i_{dr_ref} the current control references for the axis components of the GSC

i_{qr_ref} the current control references for the axis components of the GSC

v_{s_ref} the specified terminal voltage reference

P_{ref} the active power control reference

3.8.5 Model of Grid Side Controller

The GSC controller, as shown in Figure 3.8 aims to maintain the dc link voltage and control the terminal reactive power. The dc link voltage and reactive power are controlled independently via i_{dg} and i_{qg}, respectively. The Equations (3.29) to (3.34) are given as follows:

$$\frac{dx5}{d\tau} = v_{DC\_ref} - v_{DC} \tag{3.29}$$

$$i_{dg\_ref} = -K_{pdg}\Delta v_{DC} + K_{idg}\, x_5 \tag{3.30}$$

$$\frac{dx6}{d\tau} = i_{dg\_ref} - i_{dg} = -K_{pdg}\Delta v_{DC} + K_{idg}\, x_5 - i_{dg} \tag{3.31}$$

$$\frac{dx7}{d\tau} = v_{qg\_ref} - i_{dg} \tag{3.32}$$

$$\Delta v_{dg} = K_{pg}\frac{dx6}{d\tau} + K_{ig}\, x_6 = K_{pg}\left(-K_{pdg}\Delta v_{DC} + K_{idg}\, x_5 - i_{dg}\right) + K_{ig}\, x_6 \tag{3.33}$$

$$\Delta v_{qg} = K_{pg}\frac{dx7}{d\tau} + K_{ig}\, x_7 = K_{pg}(i_{qg\_ref} - i_{qg}) + K_{ig}\, x_6 \tag{3.34}$$

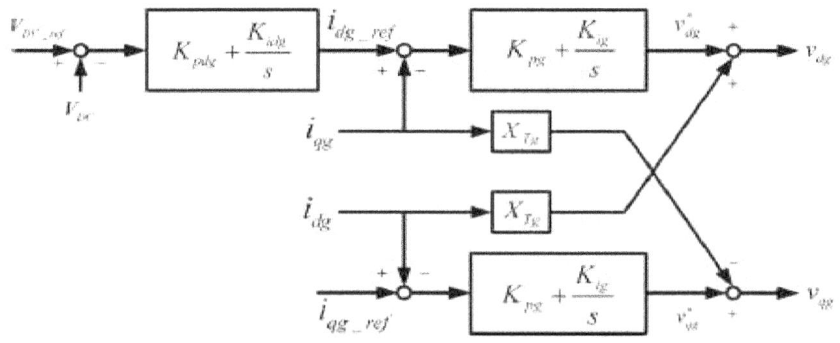

Figure 3.8 Schematic diagram of grid side controller

where,

K_{pdg} & K_{idg} the PI gains of the dc link capacitor voltage regulator

K_{pg} & K_{ig} the PI gains of the grid side converter current regulator

V_{DC_ref} the voltage control reference of the dc link capacitor

i_{qg_ref} the control reference for the axis component of the GSC current

In this research work, it is designed to be reactive neutral by setting $Q_{gc\_ref} = 0$. The grid side converter is controlled by a PI controller in such a way to guarantee a smooth DC voltage and ensure sinusoidal current in the grid side.

3.9 USE OF CONTROLLERS

The control system acts as the nervous system for the plant. It provides sensing, analysis, and control of the physical process.

When a control system is at properly tuned, the process variability is reduced, efficiency is maximized, energy costs are minimized, and production rates can be increased. Controller tuning refers to the selection of tuning parameters to ensure the best response of the controller.

3.9.1 P Controllers

P controller is mostly used in first order processes with single energy storage to stabilize the unstable process. The main usage of the P controller is to decrease the steady state error of the system. As the proportional gain factor K increases, the steady state error of the system decreases. However, despite the reduction, P control can never manage to eliminate the steady state error of the system. As we increase the proportional gain, it provides smaller amplitude and phase margin, faster dynamics satisfying wider frequency band and larger sensitivity to the noise. We can use this controller only when our system is tolerable to a constant steady state error. In addition, it can be easily concluded that applying P controller decreases the rise time and after a certain value of reduction on the steady state error, increasing K only leads to overshoot of the system response. P control also causes oscillation if sufficiently aggressive in the presence of lags and/or dead time. The more lags (higher order), the more problem it leads. Plus, it directly amplifies process noise.

3.9.2 P – D Controllers

The aim of using P-D controller is to increase the stability of the system by improving control since it has an ability to predict the future error of the system response. In order to avoid effects of the sudden change in the value of the error signal, the derivative is taken from the output response of the system variable instead of the error signal. Therefore, D mode is designed to be proportional to the change of the output variable to prevent the sudden changes occurring in the control output resulting from sudden changes in the error signal. In addition D directly amplifies process noise therefore D-only control is not used.

The value of the damping can be adjusted to achieve a critically damped response. Although PD control deals neatly with the overshoot and ringing problems associated with proportional control it does not cure the problem with the steady-state error. Fortunately it is possible to eliminate this while using relatively low gain by adding an integral term to the control function.

3.9.3 P- I - D Controllers

P-I-D Controller has the optimum control dynamics including zero steady state error, fast response (short rise time), no oscillations and higher stability. The necessity of using a derivative gain component in addition to the PI controller is to eliminate the overshoot and the oscillations occurring in the output response of the system. One of the main advantages of the P-I-D controller is that it can be used with higher order processes including more than single energy storage.

3.9.4 P- I Controllers

P-I controller is shown in Figure 3.9. It is mainly used to eliminate the steady state error resulting from P controller. However, in terms of the speed of the response and overall stability of the system, it has a negative impact. This controller is mostly used in areas where speed of the system is not an issue. Since P-I controller has no ability to predict the future errors of the system it cannot decrease the rise time and eliminate the oscillations. If applied, any amount of I guarantees set pointovershoot.

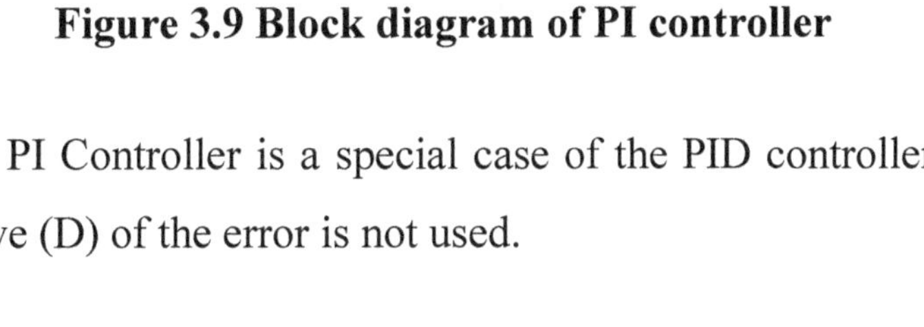

Figure 3.9 Block diagram of PI controller

A PI Controller is a special case of the PID controller in which the Derivative (D) of the error is not used.

The controller output is given by Equation (3.35).

$$K_P \Delta + K_I \int \Delta \, dt \qquad (3.35)$$

where Δ is the error or deviation of actual measured value (*PV*) from the Set Point (*SP)* Equation is (3.36).

$$\Delta = SP - PV \tag{3.36}$$

A PI controller can be modelled easily in software such as Simulink or Xcos using a "flow chart" box involving Laplace operators in Equation (3.37).

$$C = \frac{G(1+\tau s)}{\tau s} \tag{3.37}$$

where

$G = K_P$=Proportional gain

$G/T = K_I$=Integral gain

Setting a value for *G* is often a trade-off between decreasing overshoot and increasing settling time. The lack of derivative action may make the system steadier in the steady state in the case of noisy data. This is because derivative action is more sensitive to higher-frequency terms in the inputs.

3.9.5 Genetic Heuristic Controller

A stochastic control system is a control system based on stochastic logic a mathematical system that analyses analogue input values in terms of logical variables that take on continuous values between 0 and 1, in contrast to classical or digital logic, which operates on discrete values of either 1 or 0 (true or false, respectively).

The input variables in a stochastic control system are in general mapped by sets of membership functions similar to this, known as "stochastic sets". The process of converting a crisp input value to a stochastic value.

A control system may also have various types of switch, or "ON-OFF", inputs along with its analog inputs, and such switch inputs of course will always have a truth value equal to either 1 or 0, but the scheme can deal with them as simplified stochastic functions that happen to be either one value or another.

3.10 GENETIC HEURISTIC OPTIMIZATION ALGORITHM (GHO)

3.10.1 Basic Method for GHO Based Power System Stabilizer

The GHO is a stochastic global search method that mimics the metaphor of natural biological evolution. It is also an exploratory procedure that is able to locate near optimal solutions to complex problems. It maintains a set of trial solutions often called as individuals and forces them to evolve towards an acceptable solution. GHO is a four step process involving evaluation, reproduction, recombination and mutation, Goldberg (1989).

Representation Encoding of chromosomes (also called as individuals) is termed as representation which is also referred as chromosomes. In common practice chromosomes are represented by group of strings.

Step-1: Evaluation

This is the first step in each generation which is done in current chromosomes. Each chromosome in the population is decoded and evaluated on how well it solves the problem. This fitness measure is used in the next step to determine how many off springs will be generated from any particular chromosome. This represents the performance of the problem. A positive value, generally known as the fitness value, is used to reflect the degree of 'goodness' of the chromosome for solving the problem, and its value is closely related to the objective value. The design of the fitness function may vary, according to the performance requirements of the problem. The higher the fitness value, the better the system's performance. The purpose of the GHO is to manipulate the genetic operation, e.g., reproduction, crossover, or mutation, to obtain a solution corresponding to the fitness value. Basically in evaluation process individuals are selected from the populations for form pairs called parents. Selection is the key operation on GHO that ensures the survival of the fittest. 'Roulette Wheel Selection' is one of the most commonly used selection techniques.

Step-2: Reproduction

It is the process of copying individual strings according to their fitness function Copying strings according to their fitness values means that strings with the higher value has a higher probability of contributing one or more off springs in the generations.

Step-3: Recombination

Reproduction creates a population whose members currently best solve the problem. However many of the chromosomes are identical and some are different from the previous generations. Reproduction produces multiple copies of existing chromosomes from the population and produces a new chromosome that maintains many of the features of the previous generation. The most common method for recombination is crossover.

Crossover

It is a recombination operator used to vary the chromosomes from one generation to the next. Gene information at random locations between two parents or individuals is exchanged to create two new individuals called off spring which inherits the features of the parents.

Step-4: Mutation

It is an inversion of the gene in the genotype of a new member of the population. It is termed as the genetic operator used to maintain genetic diversity from one generation of a population of chromosomes to the next. It is also referred as the injection of new information into the population. The basic mutation operators that are commonly used are flipping, reversing and interchanging .Reproduction and crossover together give GHO most of their power whereas mutation helps to increase the searching power. Mutation as it does in nature, takes place very rarely on the order of once in a thousand bit string location.

3.11 PERFORMANCE ANALYSIS OF A GRID CONNECTED DFIG BASED WIND GENERATION SYSTEM WITH A PSS

3.11.1 Introduction

The system without any damping controller or PSS, and it can be observed from the time domain simulations that the oscillations are greater and the settling time for the system to be completely stable is also more. The other observations made without PSS is during the small signal stability analysis, where the state variables affect the stability of the system. In this section a PSS is developed to damp the oscillations. A small signal analysis is also carried out for the developed PSS model. It is observed that the developed system with a PSS is able to provide a more stable supply to the grid without damped oscillations and with a much less settling time.

3.12 POWER SYSTEM STABILIZER

Milad Khaleghi et al. (2011), power system stability can be defined as the property of the control system that empowers it to stay in a condition of working harmony under typical working conditions and to recapture a satisfactory condition of balance in the wake of being subjected to an unsettling influence. The main function of the PSS is to improve the system dynamic performance by providing a stable power which is done by damping the oscillation so the signals provided to the network. In conventional power plants, the PSS is used for controlling the excitation system and it is mainly employed for synchronous generators. The input signal to the PSS that are usually employed in the conventional methods are the shaft speed, terminal frequency and power, simply it can be said that auxiliary stabilizing signals are used as input signals for a PSS.

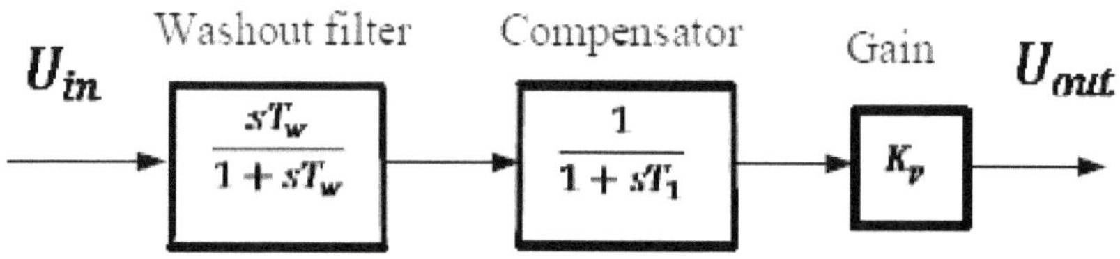

Figure 3.10 General structure of a Power System Stabilizer

In general the structure of a PSS as shown in Figure 3.10 consists of a washout filter, a proportional gain or a PI controller and a compensator block. In conventional power plants where synchronous generators generate the power, in PSS design the compensator used is a phase compensator and it is mainly used to compensate for the phase lag between the input signal and the electrical torque and it is usually a first order block. Whereas the washout filter acts as a high pass filter and it is designed to respond only to the changes in the input signal provided to it, and this do not show much effect or changes in the final output signal like voltage signals. The range of the time constant in washout filter is given in the range of 1second to 20 seconds, finally the gain determines the amount of damping introduced into PSS. As described in the value of gain is taken as high as possible and it is observed that the damping increases with the increase in the gain and beyond certain maximum value the system damping started decreasing. The time constant and the gains chosen for the current research work are discussed and are given while presenting the design aspects of PSS.

The PSS is mainly implemented in conventional power plants for synchronous generators, similar to this a PSS can be employed for a wind energy conversion system and there is a need for this, as a stable power with damped signals is required for a wind energy system to connect to the grid. Implementing PSS with wind energy conversion system is considered to be one of the new technologies in grid connected wind energy conversion system. It is mention in Gegov (1996), that presence of PSS in DFIG system improves the damping of the oscillations in the network. So this chapter mainly focused on implementing new PSS for DFIG based wind energy conversion system and a complete analysis is carried out by showing the improvements achieved on employing PSS at required points in the system.

3.13 DESIGN AND SMALL SIGNAL STABILITY ANALYSIS OF A DFIG BASED WIND SYSTEM WITH A PSS USING GHO

The most common variables that affects the stability of the system are the stator voltages and the PLL frequency $\boldsymbol{\omega}$. Even in time domain analysis it is observed that the oscillations are more due to these variables, so the PSS is employed at the points required, which are determined from small signal analysis. The newly designed PSS is able to damp the oscillations and even increase the stability of the system.

Two PSS are designed and implemented in this research work. As mentioned above the two input signals which are implemented for PSS are the stator voltage signal V_{dqs} and the PLL frequency $\boldsymbol{\omega}$pll. The two PSS's are implemented for the rotor control loops. The two PSS's are connected at the current reference signals of the rotor, i.e. at the input of the inner current control loops. The GEVS and GEFS which are introduced for a single DG system in Hong et al. (1999) are taken as base for designing the two PSS's for current research work. In this research work, both small signal analysis and the large signal time domain analysis is performed for the entire wind energy conversion system along with the PSS's. As mentioned in proper care is taken to ensure that the overall system stability is enhanced, and not just the small signal stability analysis. So the system time domain analysis is carried out and is presented.

3.13.1 Design of Voltage PSS

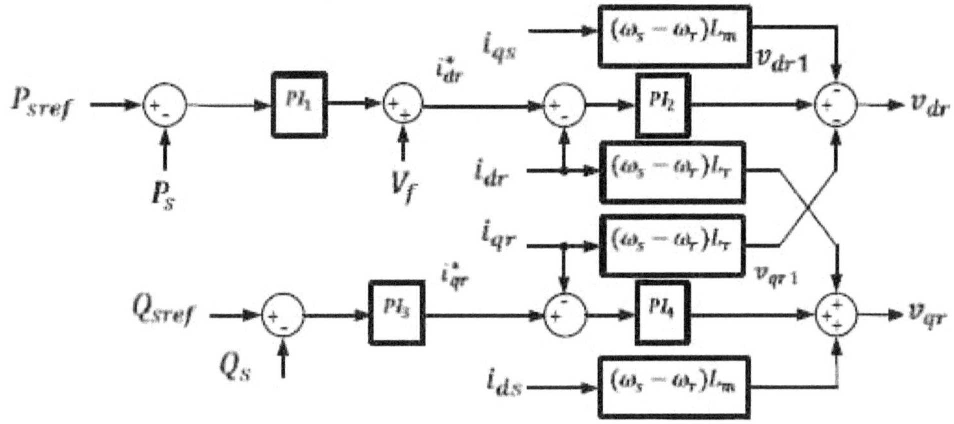

Figure 3.11 RSC with voltage PSS

In Figure 3.11 the additional signal to the RSC used in the stabilized signal v_f. The voltage of the stator is fed to this signal, as the input signal and is passed through the washout filter and the compensator and finally the output signal is obtained from the proportional gain controller which acts as the damping factor. The block diagram for the stabilizer is shown in Figure 3.12. The final output signal $v_f$is fed as the input signal to the inner current controller at the i_{dref}point along with the controlled signal of the power. The reason for employing PSS at this point is explained clearly by observing the small signal stability analysis discussed below.

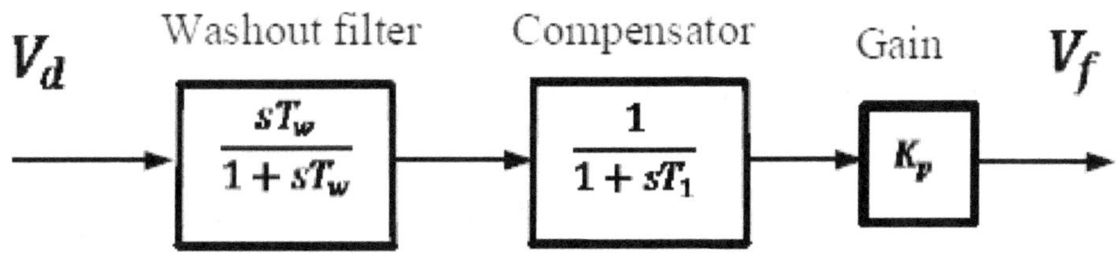

Figure 3.12 Diagram block for voltage PSS

3.13.2 Modelling of Voltage Stabilizer

From the Figure 3.12, the voltage stabilizer can be modelled and the mathematical model can be derived as Equation (3.38).,

$$V_f = V_d\left(\frac{sTw}{1+sTw}\right)\left(\frac{1}{1+sTw}\right)(K_p) \tag{3.38}$$

where,

T_w is the time constant of the washout filter and

T_l is the time constant of the compensator

K_p is the proportional gain and V_f is the output signal of PSS which is added to the inner current control loop of the rotor side converter and finally V_d is the stator voltage and it is modelled as given in Equation (3.39).

$$V_d = \sqrt{v_{ds}^2 + v_{qs}^2} \tag{3.39}$$

3.13.3 Small Signal Stability Analysis with Voltage PSS

The small signal analysis is carried out by adding this block and the linearized equations can be derived and it is expressed as given below the Equation is (3.40).

$$(\Delta V_f) + (T_w + T_1)p(\Delta V_f) = T_w K_p\, p(\Delta V_d) \tag{3.40}$$

The eigen values of (*E, A*) obtained with the developed PSS are shown in Table 3.1 and Table 3.2 the small signal stability can be analyzed.

Table 3.1 Eigen values of (*E, A*) of grid connected DFIG System with Voltage Stabilizer

	$\lambda = \sigma \pm j\omega$	σ	ω	ξ	f_{osc}
λ_1, λ_2	$-738.50 \pm 890.7i$	-738.50	890.7	0.63	141.7
λ_3	-403.03	-403.03	0	1	0
λ_4, λ_5	$-4.6 \pm 376.47i$	-4.6	376.47	0.012	59.9
λ_6, λ_7	$-69.85 \pm 364.88i$	-69.85	364.88	0.18	58.07
λ_8, λ_9	$-57.67 \pm 30.03i$	-57.67	30.03	0.88	4.7
λ_{10}	-40.67	-40.67	0	1	0
λ_{11}	-28.09	-28.09	0	1	0
$\lambda_{12}, \lambda_{13}$	$-9.45 \pm 8.39i$	-9.45	8.39	0.74	1.33
λ_{14}	-0.07	-0.07	0	1	0
$\lambda_{15}, \lambda_{16}$	$-0.51 \pm 0.7i$	-0.51	0.7	0.5812	0.1114
$\lambda_{17}, \lambda_{18}$	$-6.09 \pm 0.16i$	-6.09	0.16	0.9	0.025
λ_{19}	-0.9304	-0.9304	0	1	0
λ_{20}	-0.93012	-0.93012	0	1	0
λ_{21}	-11.14	-11.14	0	1	0

Table 3.2 Eigen values of (*E, A*) of the grid connected DFIG System with Transformation PSS

	$\lambda = \sigma \pm j\omega$	σ	ω	ξ	f_{osc}
λ_1, λ_2	$-735.81 \pm 897.7i$	-735.81	897.7	0.63	142.1
λ_3	-269.8	-269.8	0	1	0
λ_4, λ_5	$-5.02 \pm 389.67i$	-5.02	389.67	0.0129	62.07
λ_6, λ_7	$-73.54 \pm 376.36i$	-73.54	376	0.19	59.9
λ_8, λ_9	$-64 \pm 37.08i$	-64.19	37.08	0.86	5.9
λ_{10}	-40.67	-40.67	0	1	0
$\lambda_{12}, \lambda_{13}$	$-10.34 \pm 8.47i$	-10.34	8.47	0.77	1.35
λ_{14}	-0.07	-0.07	0	1	0
$\lambda_{15}, \lambda_{16}$	$-0.51 \pm 0.7i$	-0.51	0.7	0.5889	0.1114
$\lambda_{17}, \lambda_{18}$	$-6.09 \pm 0.16i$	-6.09	0.16	0.9	0.026
$\lambda_{19}, \lambda_{20}$	$-0.0019 \pm 0.93i$	-0.0019	0.93	0.002	0.15
$\lambda_{11}, \lambda_{21}$	$-16.16 \pm 1.79i$	-16.16	1.79	0.99	0.28

3.14 RESULTS AND DISCUSSION

The proposed DFIG based wind power system has been simulated and tested with MATLAB Simulink. The GHC based wind generator model with DFIG system manages to eliminates the faultswithout the use of any auxiliary hardware.The modelling and detailed analysis of the proposed model has been evaluated as follows.

3.15 SIMULATION WORK FOR OPEN LOOP

In this the DFIG is connected to the grid and there is no control system for the rotor side and a grid side converter is shown in Figure 3.13. A three phase to ground fault will be occur on the transmission line at t=3sec. The changes in the real power, reactive power, rotor speed, current and voltage waveforms are shown in below. During fault condition the real power gets changed.

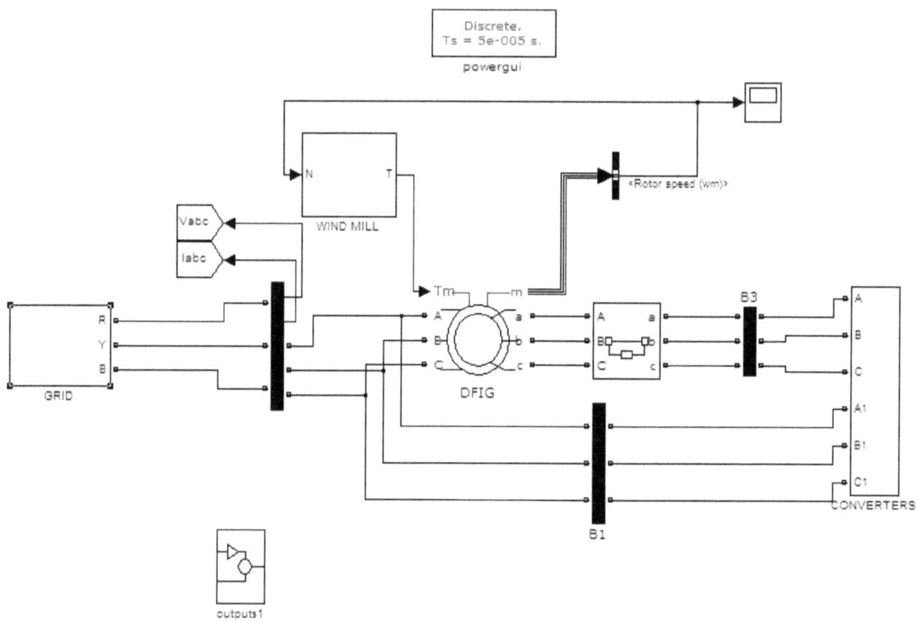

Figure 3.13 DFIG Based Wind Turbine without GH Controllers

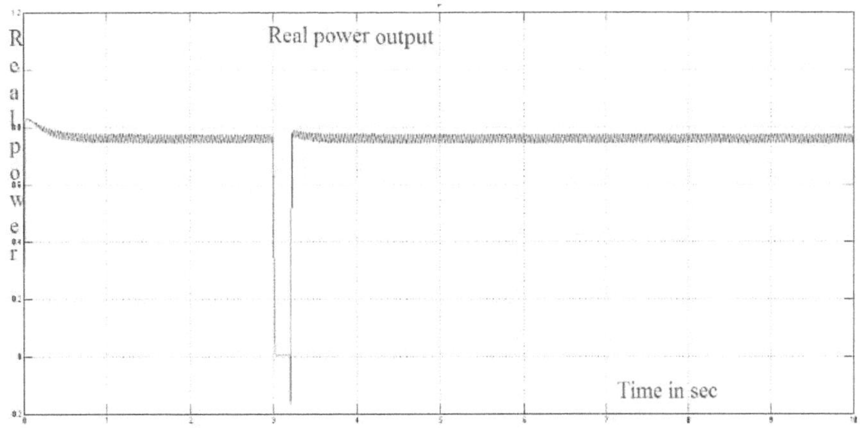

Figure 3.14 Output waveform of Real power

Figure 3.14 implies the real power flow under the three phase fault condition during that fault condition for 0.2sec. There will be dip in real power for that seconds. This leads to poor efficiency. So in order to overcome the power quality problem controllers are implemented.

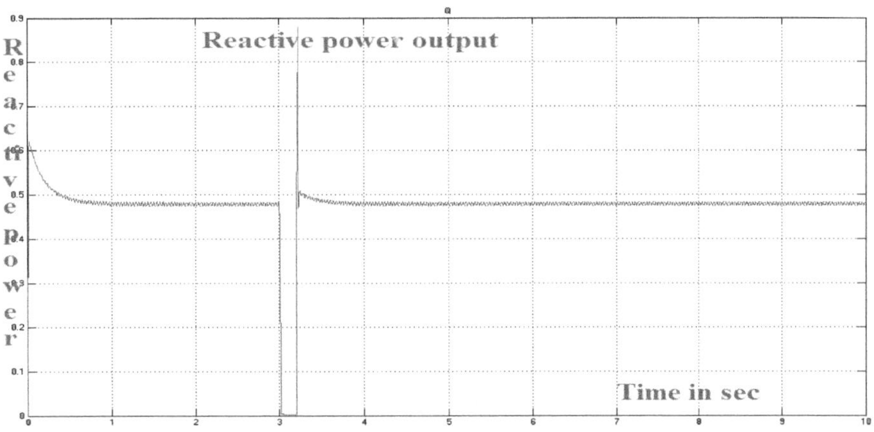

Figure 3.15 Reactive Power Output Waveform

Figure 3.15 implies the reactive power flow. Under the three phase fault condition there will be a severe fluctuation in the reactive power flow up to which the fault duration is pertained. Here fault is applied for 0.2sec.consequently reactive power will undergo a fluctuation for the same time period.

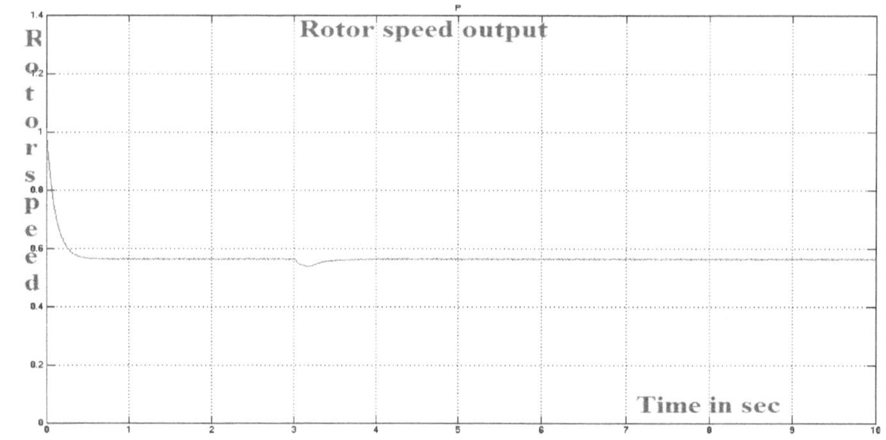

Figure 3.16 Waveform of Rotor Speed

Figure 3.16 implies the rotor speed waveform. Under the three phase fault condition there will be a severe fluctuation in the speed up to which the fault duration is pertained. Here fault is applied for 0.2sec.consequently speed will undergo a fluctuation for the same time period the thought that a signal could be changed into the type of a wavelet and afterward transformed over into its unique structure with no data loss.

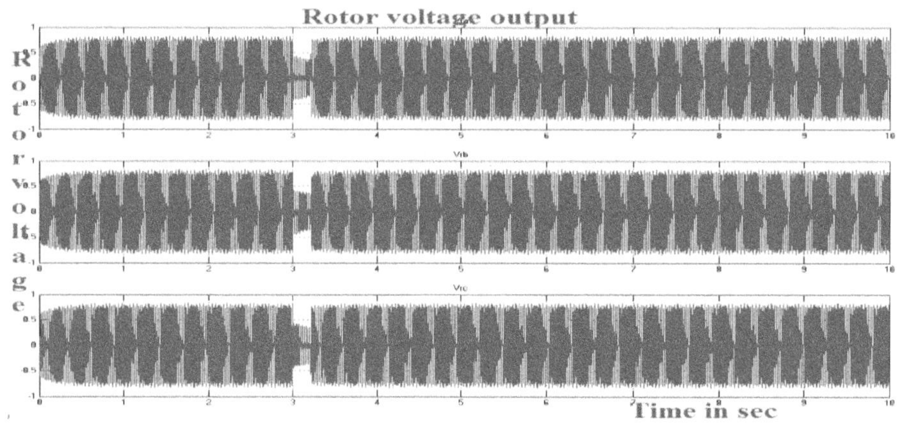

Figure 3.17 Wave form of Rotor Voltage

Figure 3.17 has the three phase rotor voltage waveform. Under the symmetrical fault condition there will be a change in the current at t=3sec., it will fluctuate for a certain period of time.

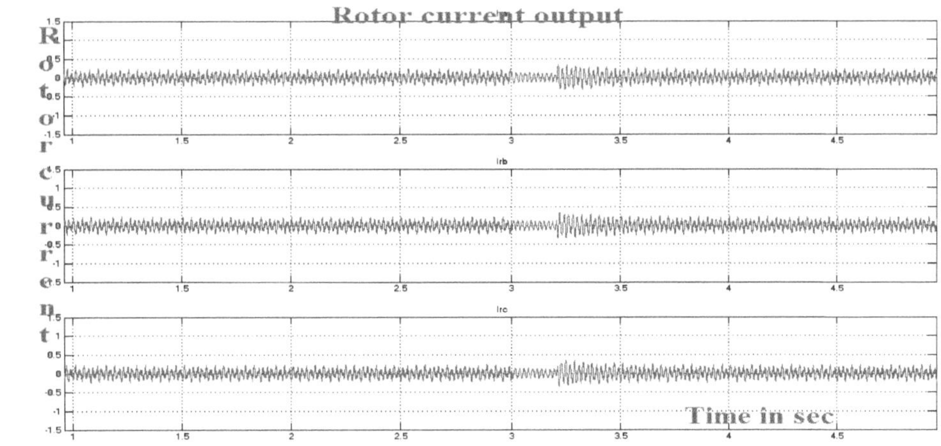

Figure 3.18 Waveform for 3 phase Rotor Current

Figure 3.18 has the three phase rotor current waveform. Under the symmetrical fault condition there will be a change in the current at t=3s, it will fluctuate for a certain period of time and shifting of a base wavelet and searching for their similarities.

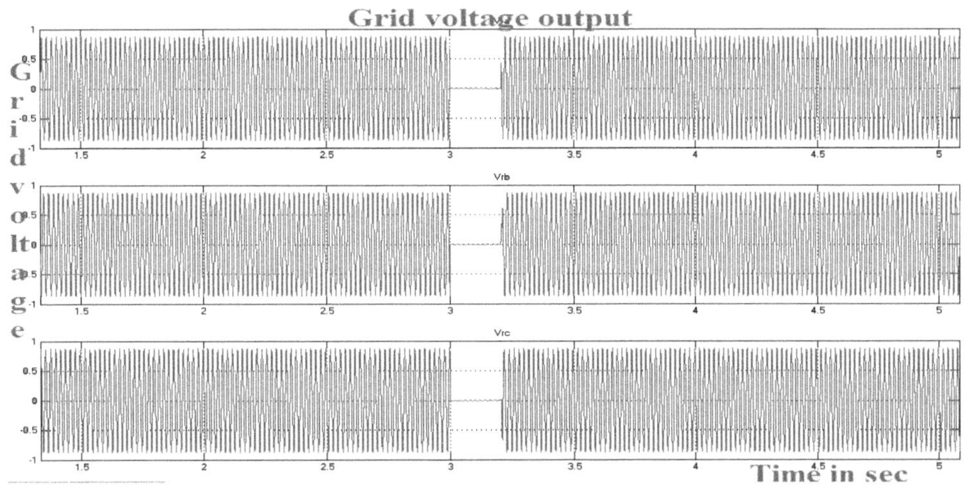

Figure 3.19 Wave form of Grid Voltage

Figure 3.19 has the three phase grid voltage waveform. Under the symmetrical fault condition there will be a change in the current at t=3s, it will fluctuate for a certain period of time.

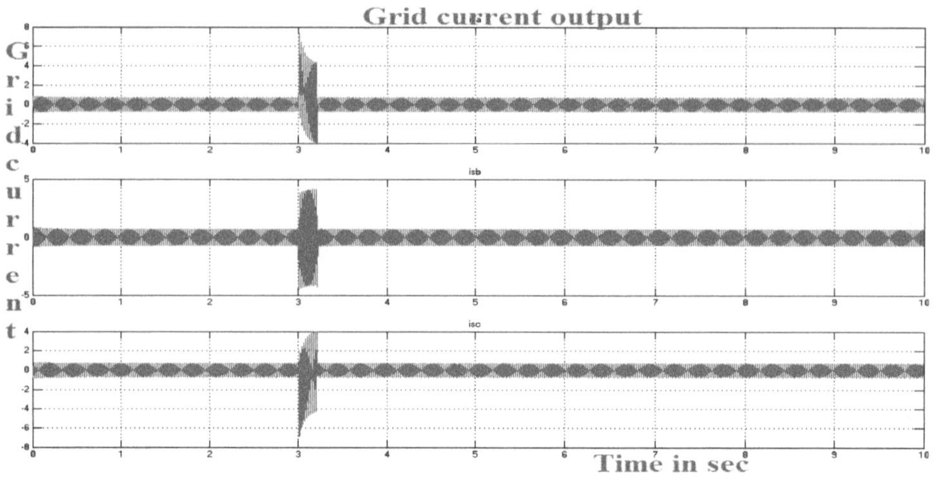

Figure 3.20 Wave form of Grid Current

Figure 3.20 has the three phase grid current waveform. Under the symmetrical fault condition there will be a change in the current at t=3sec., it will fluctuate for a certain period of time.

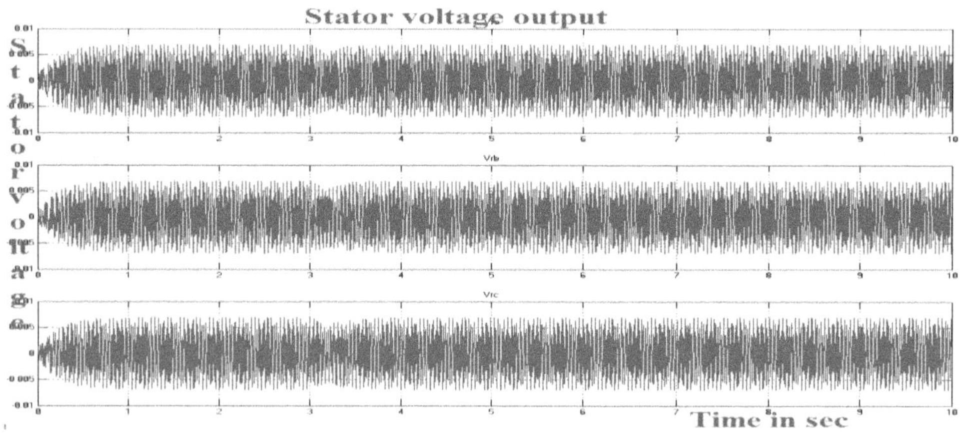

Figure 3.21 Wave form of Stator Voltage

Figure 3.21 has the three phase stator voltage waveform. Under the symmetrical fault condition there will be a change in the current at t=3sec., it will fluctuate for a certain period of time.

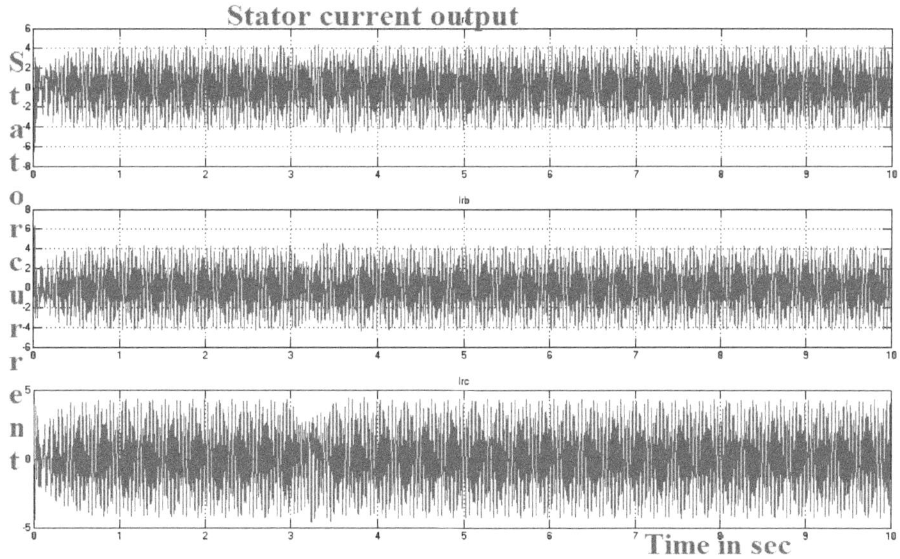

Figure 3.22 Waveform of Stator Current

Figure 3.22 has the three phase stator current waveform. Under the symmetrical fault condition there will be a change in the current at t=3sec., it will fluctuate for a certain period of time.

3.16 THEORETICAL CALCULATION OF VOLTAGE (Vabc) FFT MEASUREMENT IN OPEN LOOP

Figure 3.23 has the output voltage FFT level waveform.

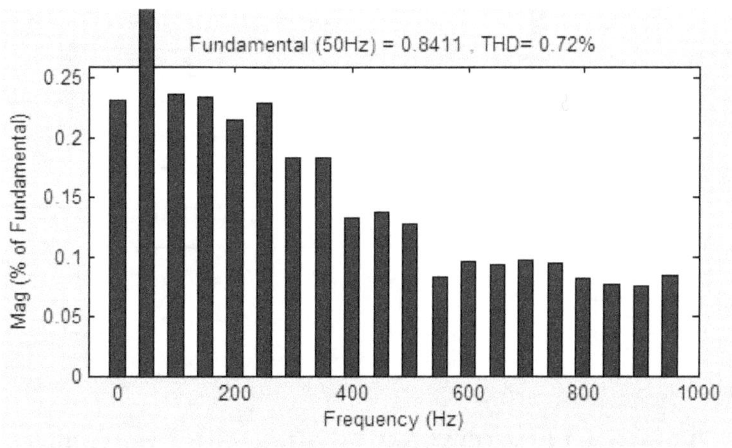

Figure 3.23 Output voltage FFT level

The THD value of vh1 to vh19 is taken from the FFT analysis of BAR Relative base value is MATLAB simulation

$$\text{THD} = \sqrt{\frac{Vn2^2 + Vn3^2 + \ldots + Vnn^2}{Vn1^2}}$$

Assume n=19

THD =

$$\sqrt{\frac{0.24^2+0.23^2+0.21^2+0.23^2+0.18^2+0.18^2+0.13^2+0.14^2+0.13^2+0.08^2+0.10^2+0.09^2+0.10^2+0.09^2+0.08^2+0.08^2+0.08^2+0.08^2}{100^2}}$$

FFT analysis value for output voltage (Vabc) (i.e.) THD = 0.0072

Therefore, Total Harmonic Distortion (THD) =0.72%.

3.17 SIMULATION WORK OF DFIG WITH GH CONTROLLERS

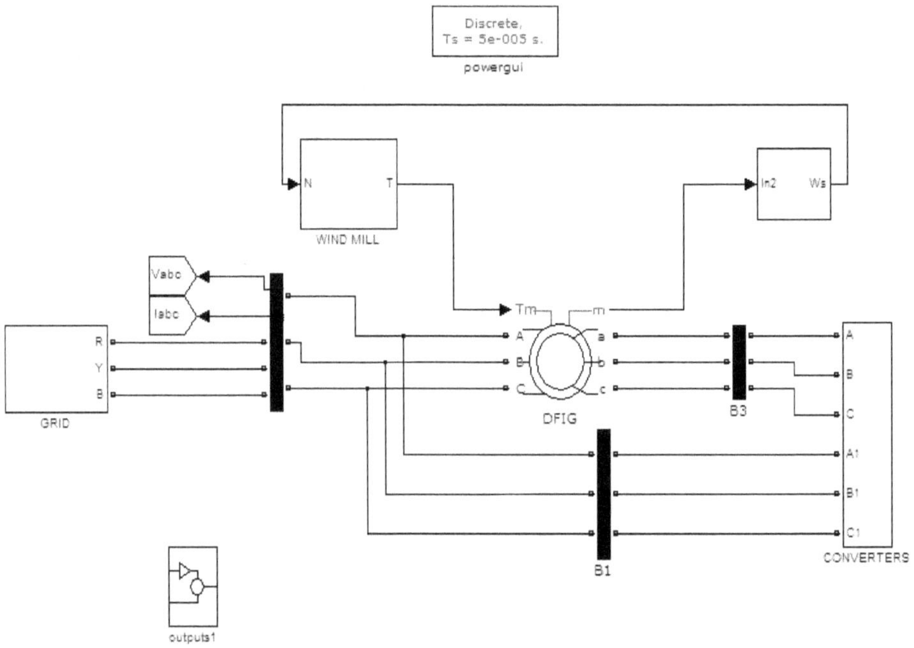

Figure 3.24 DFIG Wind Turbine with Controllers

With the proposed modification of the conventional control system, the DFIG manages to ameliorate its overall response during the fault conditions. Hence the proposed system model successfully ride through the fault, without the use of any auxiliary hardware. The research work concentrates on three phase symmetrical grid faults as shown in Figure 3.24.

3.17.1 RSC Control System

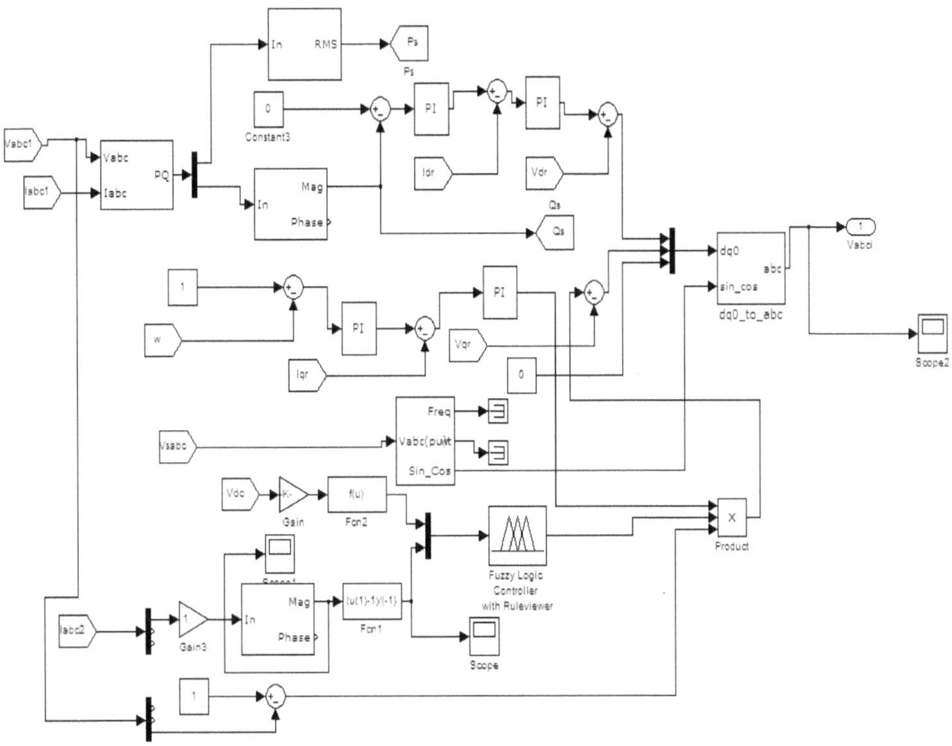

Figure 3.25 RSC with Controller

3.17.2 GSC Control System

The grid faults are controlled using RSC and GSC controllers in the system model. Above Figures 3.25 and 3.26 show the RSC and GSC controller with DFIG model.

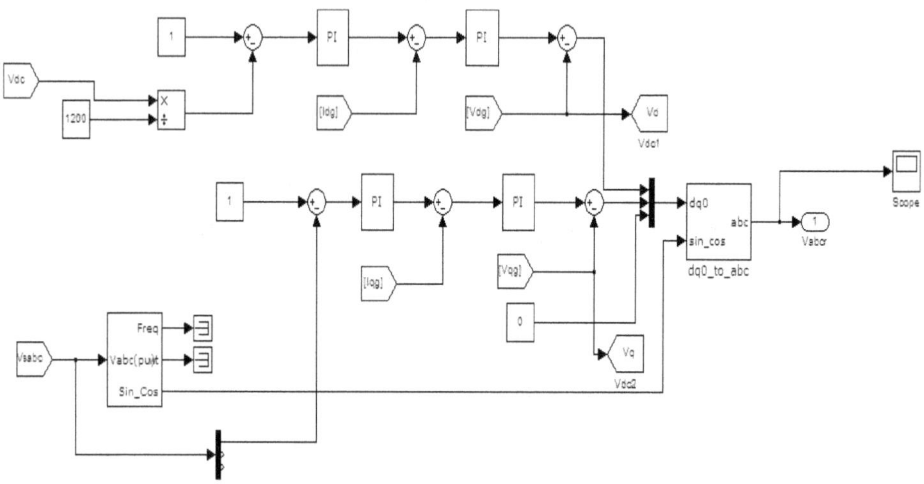

Figure 3.26 GSC with controller

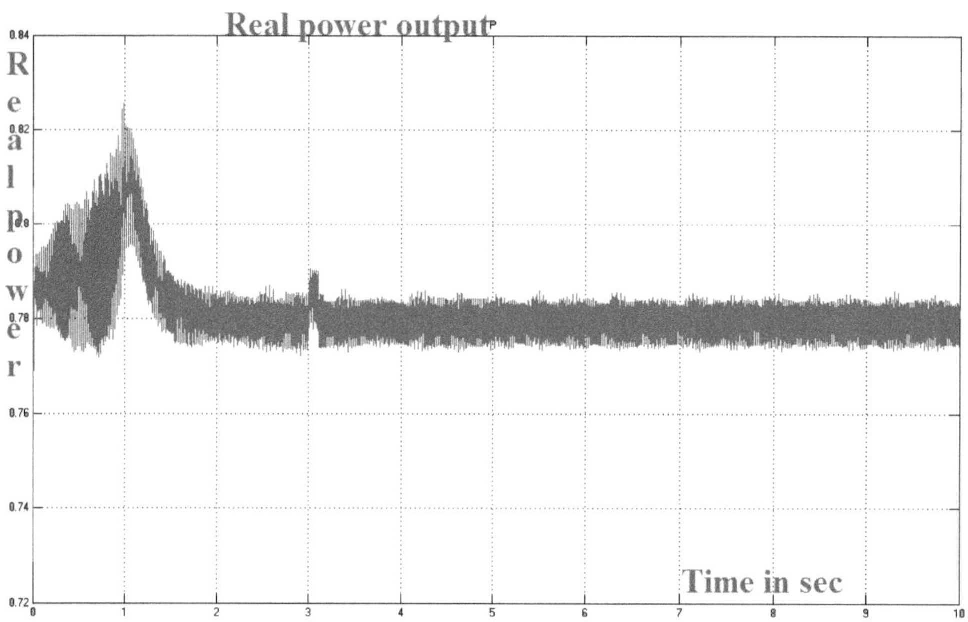

Figure 3.27 Real power output wave form

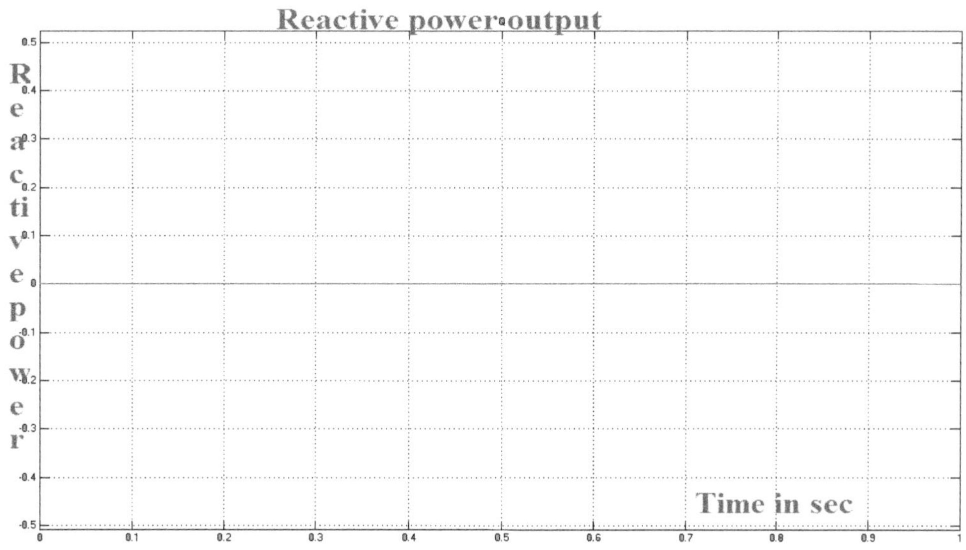

Figure 3.28 Reactive power output waveform

Figures 3.27 and 3.28 show the output waveform for real power and reactive power of Grid connected DFIG with GH controller, for the time duration of fault 3sec.From the results GH controller is used to enhance the real power under fault conditions. Hence the reactive power to set $Q_{gc} = 0$ obtain maximize active power output.

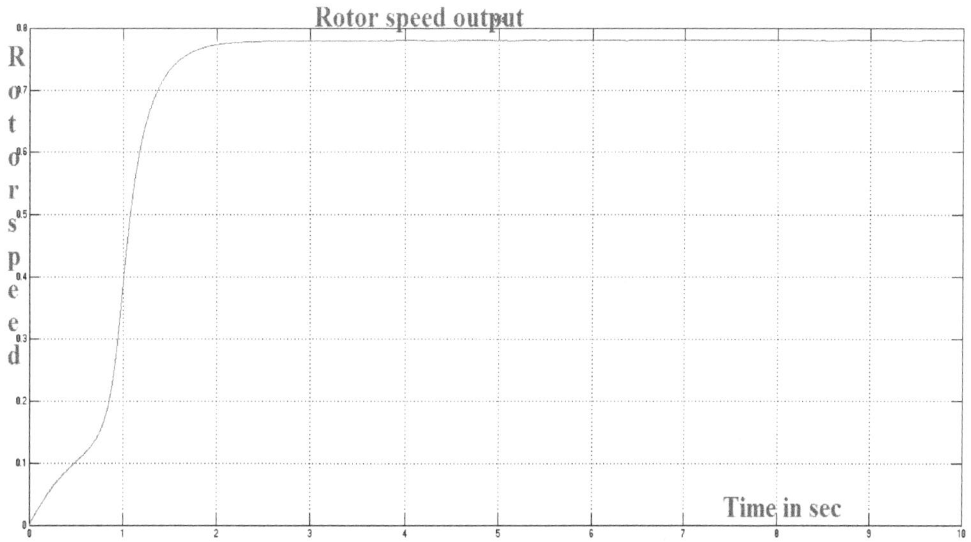

Figure 3.29 Rotor speed output wave form

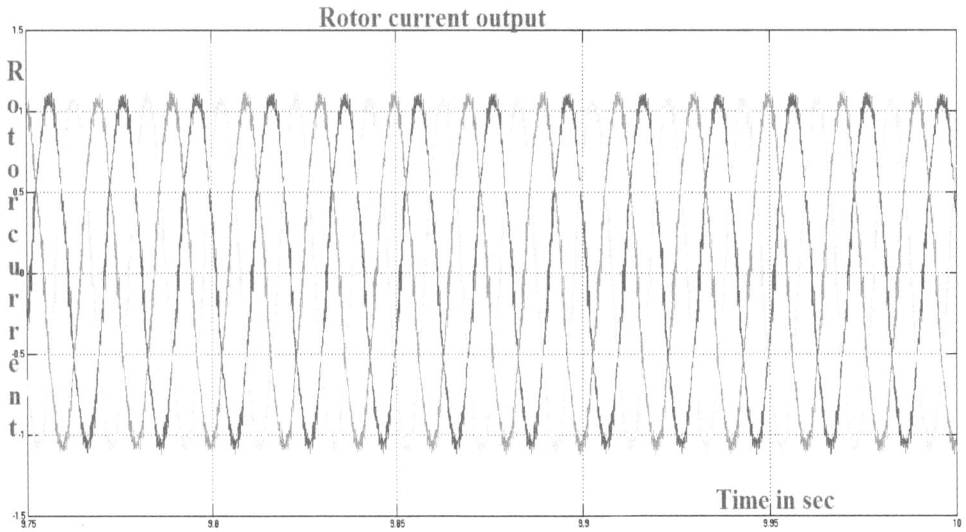

Figure 3.30 Three phase Rotor current output wave form

The above result shows the rotor speed and rotor current in Figure 3.29 and Figure 3.30 respectively. In that, according to the wind speed there will be a change in power. Due to the controller its original position attained and remains constant continuously until there is no fluctuation. Similarly the original position and remains constant in the grid voltage output shown in Figure 3.31.

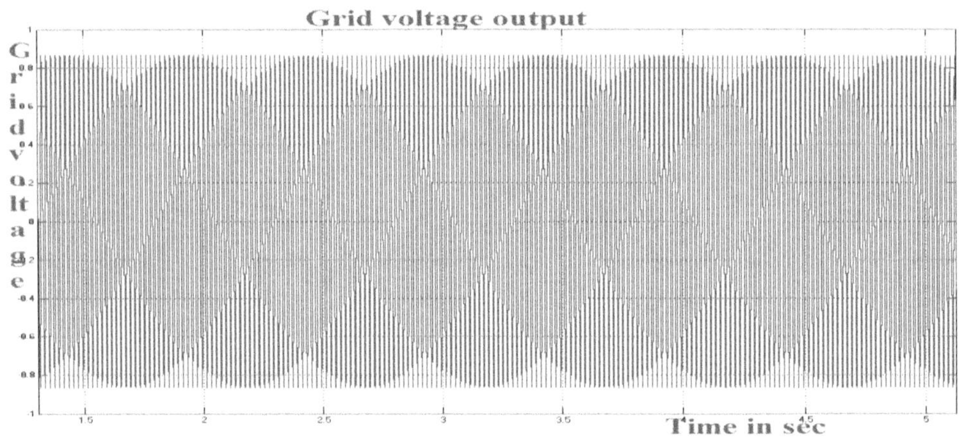

Figure 3.31 Grid voltage output wave form

3.18 FFT ANALYSIS FOR CLOSED LOOP

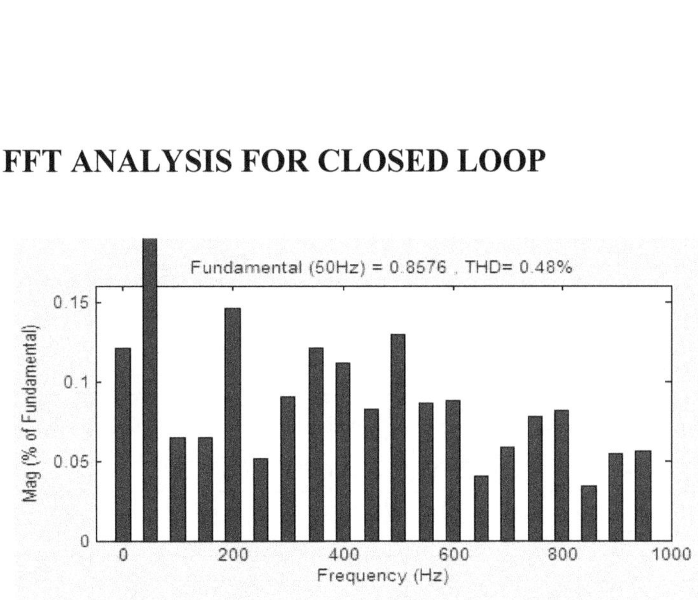

Figure 3.32 Output voltage FFT level

The THD value of vh1 to vh19 is taken from the FFT analysis of BAR Relative base value is MATLAB simulation shown in Figure 3.32.

$$\sqrt{\frac{0.06^2+0.08^2+0.06^2+0.15^2+0.09^2+0.12^2+0.11^2+0.08^2+0.13^2+0.09^2+0.09^2+0.04^2+0.06^2+0.08^2+0.03^2+0.05^2+0.06^2}{100^2}}$$

FFT analysis value for output voltage (Vabc) (ie.) THD = 0.0048

Therefore, Total Harmonic Distortion (THD) =0.48%

3.19 COMPARATIVE ANALYSIS OF PSS WITH AVR, SVC AND GHC CONTROLLERS

Table 3.3 Tuned optimal parameter values of PSS, AVR, SVC and GHC controllers

Control parameter	PSS	AVR	SVC	PROPOSED GHC
K_i / K_S	9.5721	0.7802	1.2146	1.0150
T_1 / T_{S1}	0.5243	0.3809	0.3231	0.3042
T_3 / T_{S3}	0.4385	0.4551	0.4232	0.3214

Table 3.4 Electromechanical modes and ζ under different controllers and load Conditions

No control	PSS+AVR	PSS+SVC	proposed design PSS+GHC
Normal load (λ_i, ζ_i)			
-0.3637± 8.076i, 0.0450	-1.7989±3.7059i, 0.4367	-1.7327±4.3077i, 0.3732	-2.3120±2.8779i, 0.6263
Heavy load (λ_i, ζ_i)			
-0.2562±8.2205i, 0.0312	-1.8129±3.3181i, 0.4795	-1.7647±4.7715i, 0.3469	-2.3817±2.7229i, 0.6584
Light load (λ_i, ζ_i)			
-0.4954±7.7546i, 0.0638	-1.7502±4.1483i, 0.3887	-1.7334±3.8436i, 0.4111	-2.2206±2.9599i, 0.6001
Leading PF condition (λ_i, ζ_i)			
-0.30795±6.9016i, 0.0446	-1.4306±3.434i, 0.3846	-1.6969±5.0338i, 0.3194	-2.3870±2.9806i, 0.6251

With the control parameters that are given in Table 3.3, the GHC algorithm optimal parameter values of different design controller. The test system electromechanical mode Eigen values (λi) and their damping ratios (ζi) with different control schemes and load conditions are shown in Table 3.4.

From the table, it can be observed that the system with proposed design of (PSS+GHC) provides great damping ratio than other control designs, like PSS, (PSS+AVR), and (PSS+SVC). The proposed coordinated design effectively shifts the real parts of electromechanical modes from -0.36, -0.25, -0.49 and -0.30 to -2.31, -2.38, -2.22 and -2.38 for normal, heavy, light and leading PF conditions respectively. Moreover, the damping ratios of the poorly damped electromechanical Eigen values are boosted to 0.62, 0.65, 0.60 and 0.62 for normal, heavy, light and leading PF conditions respectively. Hence, compared to other control designs, the coordinated design provides enhanced performance towards damping of electromechanical modes of the test system.

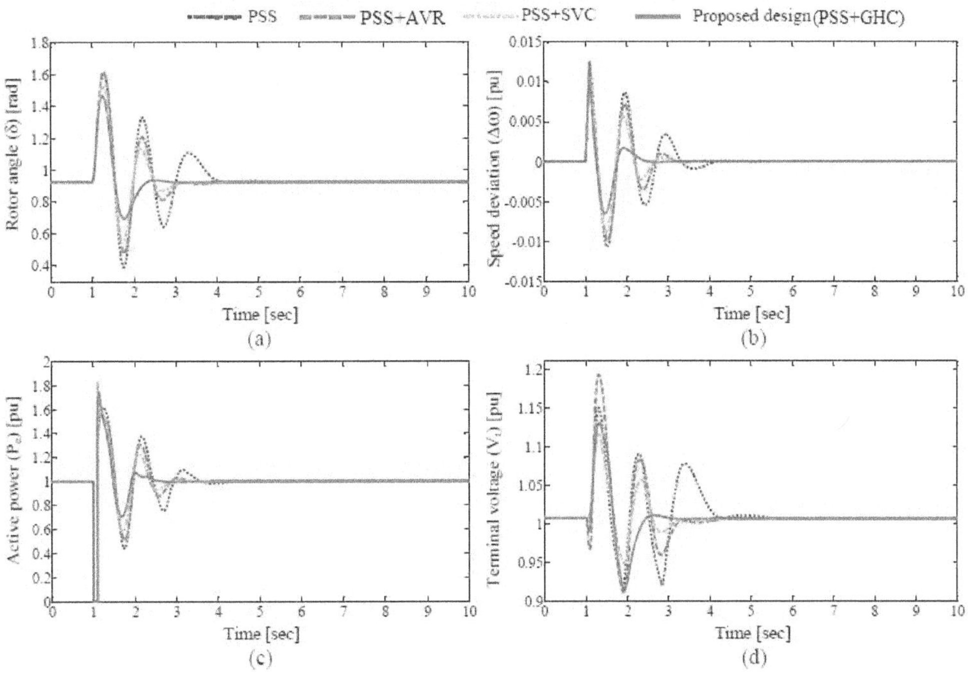

Figure 3.33 Test system dynamic response for a six cycle 3-phase fault under normal load

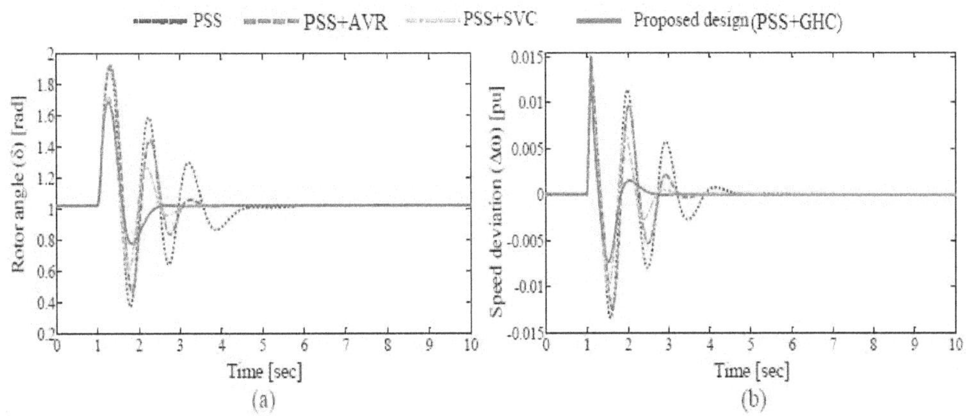

Figure 3.34 Test system dynamic response for a six cycle 3-phase fault under heavy load

The effectiveness of the performance of proposed (PSS+GHC) under severe disturbance is verified by applying a six cycle three phase fault at 1.0sec.on one of the transmission lines those are connected in between generator terminal and the infinite bus.

Figures 3.33 to 3.36 show the response of test power system due to the severe disturbance for normal, heavy, light and leading PF conditions respectively. From these figures, it is observed that the proposed hybrid coordinated design provides robust performance and achieves superior damping in comparison with the other control designs.

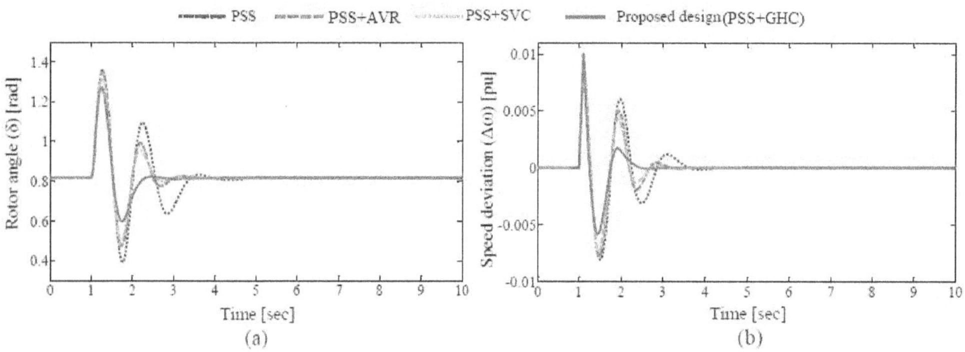

Figure 3.35 Test system dynamic response for a six cycle 3-phase fault under light load

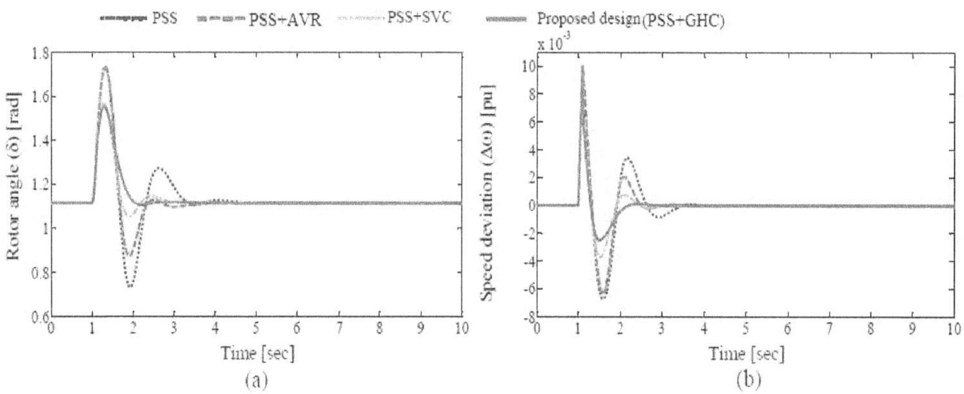

Figure 3.36 Test system dynamic response for a six cycle 3-phase fault under leading PF condition

3.20 SUMMARY

In the field of renewable energy, wind energy is one of the fastest growing and considered as the promising technology for electric power generation. From the literature review in Chapter 2, it is noticed that the contribution of wind farms to electric power grid continues to increase, majorly the DFIG based wind farms. For this reason the current research work mainly focused on DFIG based wind generation system. When integrating a wind farm into the grid one of the major issues that needs to be considered is the power system stability. By considering power system stability as the major challenge, this chapter discussed about the proposed power system stability controller Optimization and investigated the impact of the designed PSS's on the grid integrated DFIG based wind generation system. From the investigated results it is observed that the designed power system stability Genetic Heuristic Controller provide a better performance to supply a stable power to the grid. Then, the GHCO algorithm is successfully applied to find the optimal solution of the design problem. The effectiveness of proposed tuned controllers has been tested on a simple test power system through the simulation studies under different loading conditions. The Eigen value analysis and nonlinear time domain simulation results show the robustness of proposed controllers and their ability to provide good damping of system oscillations under severe disturbance.

CHAPTER 4

MODELING OF HYBRID COORDINATED CONTROLLER FOR DSTATCOM BASED POWER SYSTEM STABILIZER

4.1 INTRODUCTION

General modelling and optimal design of Hybrid Coordinated Controller (HCC) used for FACTS controllers, their effectiveness and robustness for a fault disturbance over a wide range of operating conditions based system is discussed here. In this chapter, the Hybrid Coordinated Controller (HCC) design of PSS and DSTACOM based Hybrid controllers are analyzed in detail. In this chapter, the modelling of HCC design with POD, PSS, with DSTATCOM controllers and their optimal designs with POD stabilizers is considered. Knowledge of the characteristics and modelling of individual system components as discussed in Chapter 2 is helpful in this analysis. The synchronized designing problem is formulated as an optimization problem and the objective function of this optimization problem is evaluated using Hybrid Coordinated Controller Optimization (HCC) algorithm. Knowledge of the modelling and operation of PSS with power system and basic design of DSTACOM based FACTS damping controller are helpful in this synchronized controller design analysis.

4.2 PROBLEMS IDENTIFIED IN THE PREVIOUS METHODS

In this section a literature survey related to power system oscillations and control measures to damp these oscillations is highlighted. The power system may be thought as a large interconnected and complex system with many lightly damped electromechanical mode of oscillations. The mechanical inertia and power angle characteristics led to oscillations of 1- 3Hz observed in hydro generators at light load, when they operated in parallel. During such oscillations, mechanical kinetic energy is exchanged in the form of electric power between synchronous generators and the network. The speed governors are able to preserve the frequency stability but they cannot guarantee the damping of oscillations among paralleled generators.

4.2.1 Conventional Control Methods

De Mello& Concordia (1969) used Single Machine Infinite Bus (SMIB) system to analyze the nature of the low frequency electromechanical oscillations in power systems. They were the first to explain the phenomena of oscillations by the concepts of synchronous and damping torques, and stated that inadequate damping torque is the reason for oscillations or instability of power system. The excitation controller design has drawn sizable consideration to control synchronous generator and stabilize power system oscillations. Here, the operation of excitation control continues to maintain generator voltage and reactive power output. A high response exciter is helpful in adding synchronizing torque. However, on account of performing, it introduces damping. One of the conventional efficient methods to meet the conflicting exciter behaviour with respect to system stability is to install a PSS. The basic function of a

PSS is to produce an auxiliary stabilizing signal to make electrical torque component in phase with speed variations.

In past two decades, enormous research being conducted on designing of PSS for power system stability enhancement. Different methods like linear design methods, nonlinear designing methods and intelligent optimization methods have been proposed. A robust PSS designed by shifting the real parts of poles to any desired positions while preserving the imaginary parts. Using differential geometric linearization approach PSS is designed in a multi-machine system enhances the power system damping under multi-operating conditions probabilistic eigen value sensitivity based PSS. The optimal control algorithm like simple Fuzzy Logic Controller (FLC) which applied for adaptive PSS design in SMIB system.

The dynamic output feedback model based fuzzy PSS is designed for robust performance of power system. Many modern heuristic optimization techniques (such as genetic algorithms (GA), Simulated Annealing (SA), Particle Swarm Optimization (PSO), Bacterial Foraging Optimization (BFO), DE etc.,) were introduced and have been successfully applied for design of PSSs to improve the power system dynamic stability.

However, with increasing the transmission line loading over very long distance in a multi machine system, these PSSs cannot guarantee the damping of inter-area oscillations if the operating conditions vary abruptly. Additionally, PSS can cause great variations in the voltage profile under severe disturbances and they may even result in leading Power Factor (PF) operation, which causes losing system stability. In such scenarios, it would be feasible to install Distributed STATCOM based FACTS controllers that were proposed.

4.3 FACTS CONTROLLERS

The last few years, FACTS controllers have great research interest due to their versatile capability in power system stability issues. FACTS controllers have been extensively studied and analyzed for various power system problems such as power flow control, power transfer capability enhancement, voltage regulation, enhancing power system stability and damping the power system oscillations. Here, a brief review is given for the FACTS controllers like STATCOM and DSTATCOM applied for power system stability and damping of power oscillations problems.

4.3.1 Static Synchronous Compensator (STATCOM)

The emergence of FACTS devices and in particular GTO thyristor-based STATCOM has enabled such technology to be proposed as serious competitive alternatives to conventional SVC. From the viewpoint of power system dynamic stability, the STATCOM provides better damping characteristics than the SVC as it is able to transiently exchange active power with the system. Abido (1999) presented a Singular Value Decomposition (SVD) based approach to assess and measure the controllability of the poorly damped electromechanical modes by STATCOM. It was observed that the electromechanical modes are more controllable via phase modulation channel. It was also concluded that the STATCOM-based damping stabilizers extend the critical clearing time and enhance greatly the power system transient stability. Haque demonstrated that by the use of energy function, a STATCOM can provide additional damping torque to the low frequency oscillations in a power system.

A STATCOM based variable structure for power system oscillations damping are discussed earlier. STATCOM consists of two internal controllers of STATCOM namely AC and DC voltage controllers. Moreover, it is reported that the joint operation of these internal controllers could produce HCC interactions. The application of FACTS to power system stability in particular, has a tremendous increment. In summary, the performance analysis of above mentioned FACTS controllers and the first column of Table 4.1 shows that FACTS controller like DSTATCOM is good for load flow control.

Table 4.1 Performance analysis of FACTS controllers

FACTS Controller	Load flow control	Voltage stability	Transient stability	Dynamic stability
SVC	★	★★★	★	★★
STATCOM	★	★★★	★★	★★
DSTATCOM	★★	★	★★★	★★

While, shunt connected controllers like SVC and STATCOM have great voltage stability performance. Whereas DSTATCOM controller has very good transient stability performance compared to all other controllers. In case of dynamic stability all controllers perform well. Hence, to enhance the overall stability of the power system and to damp the power system oscillations, combined effect of these series and shunt controllers is much needed.

4.3.2 Coordination of PSS and FACTS Controllers

The internal controllers like PSSs are mounted on the generators, can damp the local mode of oscillations effectively, but they cannot promise sufficient damping to inter-area mode of oscillations. In such cases, the external controllers like FACTS controllers, are installed in the power transmission network help to provide sufficient damping to inter-area mode of oscillations. Therefore, the coordination of PSS and FACTS controllers is needed to damp all types of power system oscillations effectively.

In recent past, numerous publications reported the coordination of PSS and FACTS damping controllers for maintaining or enhancing electromechanical oscillations damping in power systems. The synchronized design of PSS with DSTACOM using phase compensation method is discussed and decentralized state feedback control method.

From the above research background, we summarized that the use of PSS can provide good damping to local mode of oscillations and FACTS controllers can provide good damping to inter-area mode of oscillations. By the help of series FACTS controllers the transient stability of the system is greatly enhanced, with the help of shunt FACTS controllers one can maintain voltage stability of the system. Hence, to damp local as well as inter-area mode of oscillations and to enhance overall system dynamic performance a hybrid synchronized design of PSS with series and shunt FACTS damping controllers is required. Moreover, from the considered literature the validation of coordination design in real-time not exist till date. DSTATCOM controllers are used to overcome the above challenges and to demonstrate the innovative design in this Chapter.

4.3.3 Modelling of DSTATCOM Controllers

The modelling aspects of DSTATCOM based FACTS controllers are discussed in brief manner for damping of power oscillations.

The basic structure of DSTATCOM is connected to a bus *S* with voltage *VS* through a transformer of leakage reactance *Xs*. The DSTATCOM consists of a 3-phase Voltage Source Converter (VSC) and a

DC capacitor with capacitance C_{DC}. The VSC converts DC voltage $V_{DC}$to a controllable AC voltage V_m at an angle α_s. Due to the difference between these two voltages, there is a power exchange between STATCOM and the power system. Hence, by adjusting the values of voltage magnitude V_m and the phase angle α_s we can control the power flow. From Figure 4.1, the control Equations (4.1) and (4.2) of DSTATCOM are given by

$$V_m = kmV_{DC}(\cos\alpha_s + j\sin\alpha_s) = \mathrm{kmV}_{DC}\angle\alpha_s \quad (4.1)$$

$$\dot{V}_{DC} = \frac{km}{C_{DC}}(\mathrm{I}_{Sd}\cos\alpha_s + \mathrm{I}_{Sq}\sin\alpha_s) \quad (4.2)$$

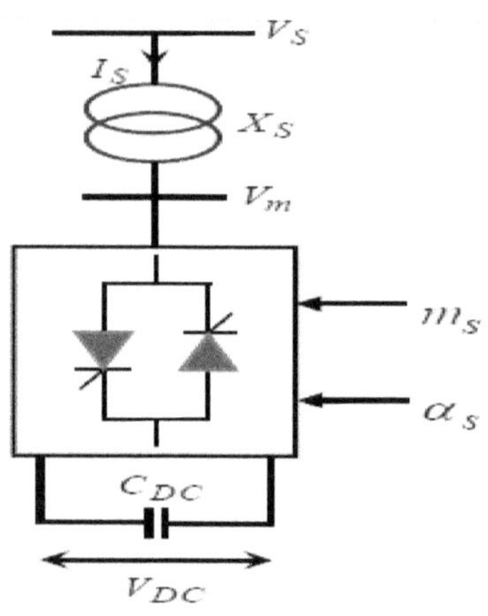

Figure 4.1 Structure of DSTATCOM

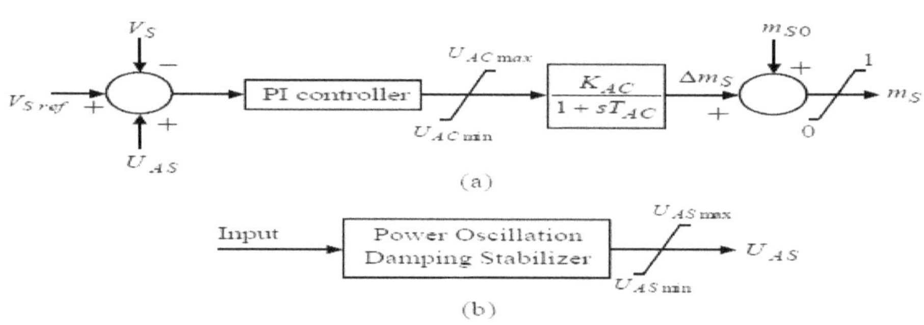

Figure 4.2 (a) PI based AC voltage controller and (b) additional POD stabilizer of the DSTATCOM

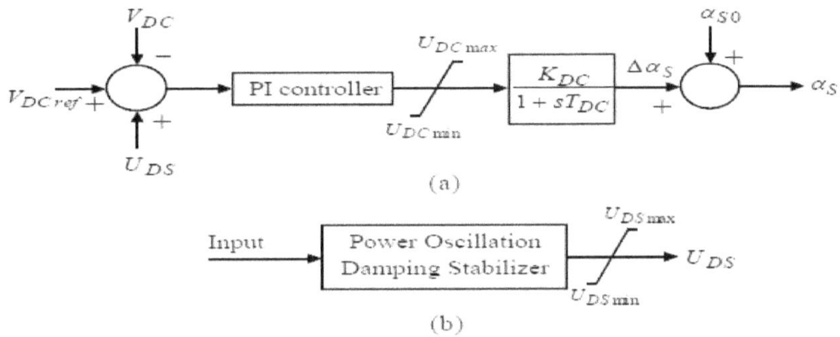

Figure 4.3 (a) PI based DC voltage controller and (b) additional POD stabilizer of the DSTATCOM

The internal controllers of DSTATCOM are designed with PI based controller, Figure 4.2(a) shows the PI based DSTATCOM AC voltage controller. The difference in AC voltage V_S and its reference value is considered as input of the controller. Here, one more additional input U_{AS} is also taken from POD based PSS, which is shown in Figure 4.2 (b). The PI based AC voltage controller with HCC ins K_{PAC} and K_{IAC} gives modulation index as output. On the other hand, in Figure 4.3 (a), the difference of DC voltage of the capacitor V_{DC} and its reference value is given as input to the PI based DC voltage controller and in addition to these two inputs, the output of damping controller is also fed as input as shown in Figure 4.3 (b).

4.4 STRUCTURE OF HYBRID COORDINATED CONTROLLER (HCC) BASED POD STABILIZERS

The power oscillations damping stabilizers give additional damping signal to the DSTATCOM controllers such that they can be able to damp the power system oscillations quickly under disturbance. Recently, several advanced control design approaches based on optimal control, robust control, adaptive control and intelligent control have been developed for power system oscillation damping. In spite of the merits of such advanced controls, many industries and power system utilities still prefer simple PID and Lead-lag based damping controller structures. Here, to analyze the performance of power system under disturbance, the following control structures are discussed.

- HCC with PID controller based POD stabilizers.
- HCC with Lead-Lag controller based POD stabilizers.

4.4.1 Structure of HCC with PID Controller Based POD Stabilizers

Over past 50 years, the PID controller is most widely used as a feedback controller in many industries. It is a simple, robust, easily realizable and cost effective controller that can provide excellent control performance despite the varied dynamic characteristics of power plant. As the name indicates, PID controller is integration of three basic controllers, those are proportional, integral and derivative controllers. Each controller has their own effect to stabilize the output of the plant. The proportional controller helps to reduce the rise time, but it never eliminates the steady-state error. By this reason, if the proportional PSO in is too high, then the system becomes unstable where as a small PSO in brings about a little yield reaction to a substantial info blunder and less sensitive Jalilvand & Daviran Keshavarzi (2010). The integral controller can eliminate steady-state error, whereas it makes the transient response too worse. High integral Inter Weed Optimization (IWO) can cause overshoot and low value will make system response sluggish. The derivative controller will help to improve the stability of the system, reduce the overshoot and increase the transient response. If the derivative PSO in is sufficiently high it can cause system unstable and it makes more noise. Conventional fixed PSO in PID controller is widely used for control process in power industries. In the design of this Hybrid coordinated controller one has to set three main parameters proportional HCCO in (K_P), integral HCCO in (K_I) and derivative HCCO in (K_D). Mostly, the HCC controllers are tuned by the trial and error method based on the experience over plant behaviour. The block diagram of HCC based PID controller Ruhua et al. (2003), for a closed loop system is shown in Figure 4.4 and the transfer function is represented by Equation (4.3).

$$G_{PID} = K_P + \frac{K_I}{S} + sK_D \tag{4.3}$$

The output of PID controller in time domain is given by Equation (4.4).

$$u(t) = K_P e(t) + K_I \int e(t)\, dt + K_D \frac{de(t)}{dt} \tag{4.4}$$

where $u(t)$ is control signal and $e(t)$ is error signal.

In this research work, the DSTATCOM based POD stabilizers are designed by using PID based controllers. Figure 4.5 represents the structure of HCC with PID controller based FACTS POD stabilizers. The input signal given to POD stabilizers depend on the type of FACTS controller. In general, for series controllers change in the line active power is given as input signal whereas for shunt connected DSTATCOM controllers change in bus voltage is given as input signal. The output signal of POD stabilizer is also given as one more input to the DSTATCOM controller.

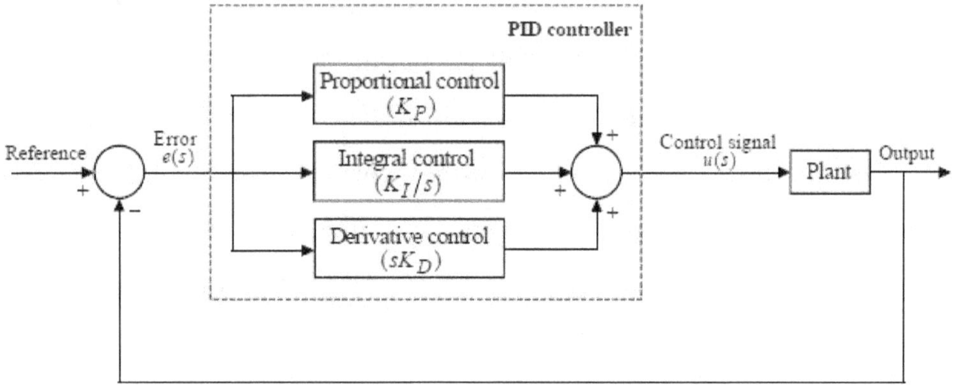

Figure 4.4 Block diagram representation of HCC - PID controller

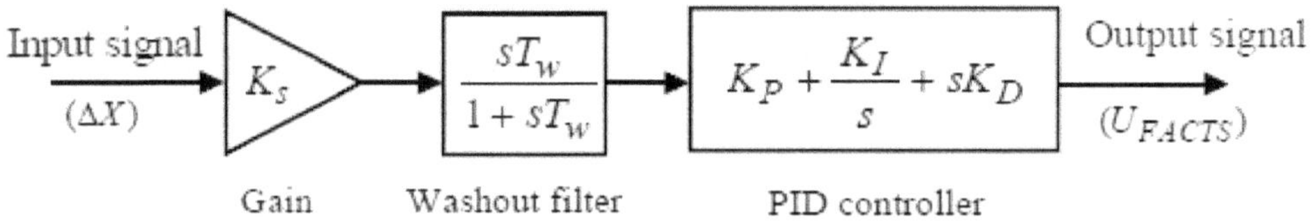

Figure 4.5 Structure of HCC controller based POD stabilizer

For the proper design of HCC controllers, the parameters of PID controller such as K_P, K_I and K_D must be selected by some suitable tuning method to improve the transient response and minimize the steady state error.

4.4.2 Structure of HCC with Lead-Lag Controller Based POD Stabilizers

The Lead-Lag controller is simple yet effective controller, which is commonly used in many industries for error compensation. For the design of a Lead-Lag compensator (or controller), an engineer much consider whether the system needs Lead-compensator, Lag-compensator, or a combination of the two. Lead compensation essentially yields an appropriate improvement in transient response and a little improvement in steady state accuracy. On the other hand, Lag compensation yields an appreciable enhancement in steady state accuracy at the expense of increasing the transient response time. The Lead-Lag compensation combines the characteristics of both lead compensation and lag compensation. Hence, Lead-Lag controller can improve system parameters such as reducing steady state error, reducing resonant peak, improving system transient response by reducing the rise time. The basic block diagram of two stage HCC – Lead-Lag controller is shown in Figure 4.6 and the transfer function is given by Equation (4.5).

$$G_{LL} = \frac{(1+sT_1)(1+sT_3)}{(1+sT_2)(1+sT_4)} \tag{4.5}$$

where, T_1, T_2, T_3 and T_4 are time constants of Lead-Lag controller.

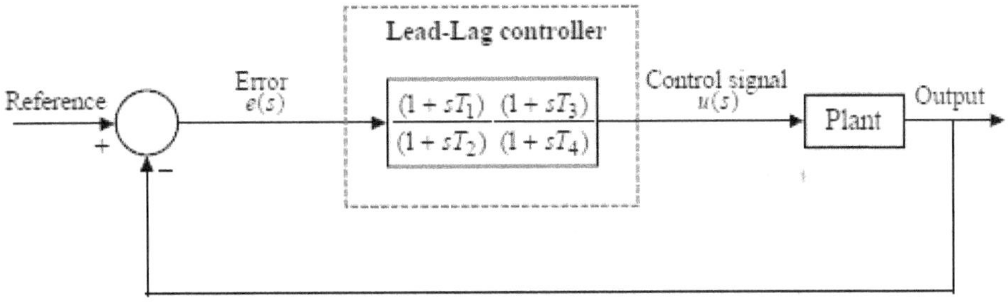

Figure 4.6 Block diagram representation of HCC-Lead-Lag controller

The Lead-Lag controller provides lead compensation if the numerator time constants are greater than denominator time constants. Similarly, it provides lag compensation if time constants of numerator are lesser than time constants of denominator. Figure 4.7 represents the structure of HCC - Lead-Lag controller based POD stabilizer.

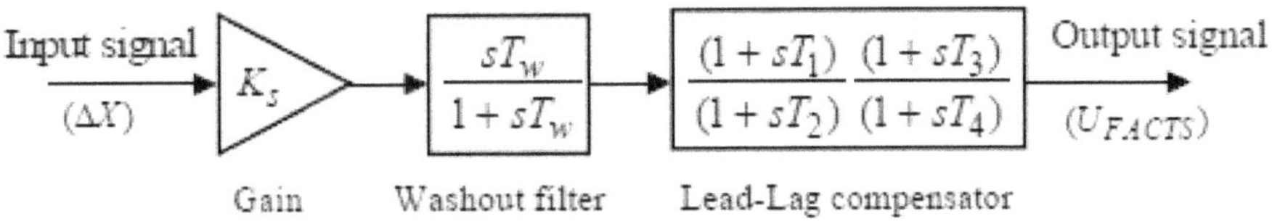

Figure 4.7 Structure of HCC-Lead-Lag controller based POD stabilizer

To improve the dynamic response and to damp the power system oscillations, proper tuning of control parameters associated with these POD stabilizers is requisite. Several techniques have been proposed for tuning of control parameters in POD stabilizers. In this research work, Hybrid coordinated Controller Optimization (HCCO) is used to find the optimal control parameters of different POD stabilizers.

4.5 HYBRID COORDINATED CONTROLLER OPTIMIZATION ALGORITHM (HCCO)

The algorithmic steps for general HCCO Based DSTATCOM Problems are as follows:

Step-1: Creation of initial population

The initial vector population is chosen randomly and should cover then tire parameter space. Every person in the hereditary populace speaks to an applicant arrangement. For tuning of HCC with PSS controller, the elements of the solution consist of, Stabilizer gain (K_S), Time constants of compensator(T_1, T_2, T_3, T_4) and Washout time constant (T_W). These factors are spoken to as gliding point numbers in the multi-machine population. The parameters governing the system are presented in a vector form as PV= $[K_S, T_1, T_2, T_3, T_4, T_W]^T$, each parameter K_i is a real number. HCCO searches a global optimum point in N-dimensional search space. It initializes the parameter vector randomly under uniform probability distribution within the search space constrained by the prescribed minimum and maximum bounds as in Equation (4.6).

$$K_{si}^{0} = K_{si(\min)} + \text{rand}.\left(K_{si\,(\max)} - K_{si(\min)}\right) \quad (4.6)$$

$$T_i^{0} = T_{i(\min)} + \text{rand}.\left(T_{i(\max)} - T_{i\,(\min)}\right)$$

where K_i (min) and K_i (max) are lower and upper limit of object vectors respectively. The parameter vectors are the bounded values of the control variables (HCC parameters) that are distributed in a constrained solution space.

$$\left.\begin{array}{l} K_{si}^{\min} \le K_{si} \le K_{si}^{\max} \\ T_{1i}^{\min} \le T_{1i} \le T_{1i}^{\max} \\ T_{2i}^{\min} \le T_{2i} \le T_{2i}^{\max} \\ T_{3i}^{\min} \le T_{3i} \le T_{3i}^{\max} \\ T_{4i}^{\min} \le T_{4i} \le T_{4i}^{\max} \\ T_{wi}^{\min} \le T_{wi} \le T_{wi}^{\max} \end{array}\right\} \tag{4.7}$$

The proposed approach make use of GHCO to tackle this streamlining issue and look for ideal or close ideal arrangement of HCCO parameters { T1i, T2i, T3i, T4i, Twi, KSi}; i= {1, 2, 3,... m},where *m* is the number of machines as shown in Equation in (4.7).

Step-2: Fitness Function

Each parameter set is used to evaluate the objective function value of the individuals in the population. The objective function calculation can be estimated using the fitness function of the individual. Fitter chromosomes have higher probabilities of being selected for the next generation. The fitness function is the reciprocal of the performance criterion. Hence, the minimization of objective function given by Equation 4.8 is transformed to a fitness function to be maximized as

$$objective\ function\ J = \sum_{j-1}^{NP} \sum_{\sigma_1 \ge \sigma_0 -} (\sigma_0 - \sigma_1)^2 + \alpha \times \sum_{j\,1}^{NP} \sum_{\varsigma_1 \le \varsigma_0} (\varsigma_0 - \varsigma)_i^2 \tag{4.8}$$

Step-3: Mutation

For each target vector K_i, G and T_i, G of the generation 'G' , a mutant vector K_{mi},G+1 and T_{mi},G+1 is generated according to the following equation with random indexes r1, r2, r3 € {1,2,....NP} This basic form of this equation is given in the above reference Ching et al. (2011).

$$K_{mi,}G+\mathbf{1} = K_{r1,}G + F_1.(\mathrm{K}_{r\mathbf{2},G} - \mathrm{K}_{r\mathbf{3},G}) + \mathrm{F}_\mathbf{2}.(\mathrm{K}_{best} - \mathrm{K}_{pi,G}) + \mathrm{F}_\mathbf{3}.(\mathrm{K}_{pi,G} - \mathrm{K}_{pi,G-\mathbf{1}})$$
$$T_{mi,}G+\mathbf{1} = T_{r1,}G + F_1.(\mathrm{T}_{r\mathbf{2},G} - T_{r\mathbf{3},G}) + \mathrm{F}_\mathbf{2}.(\mathrm{T}_{best} - T_{pi,G}) + \mathrm{F}_\mathbf{3}.(\mathrm{T}_{pi,G} - T_{pi,G-\mathbf{1}}) \quad (4.9)$$

where NP represents the number of population and is always ≥ 4. F_1, F_2, F_3 € [0, 1] are the scaling factors (or mutation factors) and p≠ r1≠ r2.

K_{best}, K_{pi}, G, K_{pi}, G - K_{pi}, G-1 represents the best individual vector, each individual vector and the momentum term respectively.

Thus HCCO generates new parameter vectors by adding the weighted difference between two population vectors to a third vector called mutated vector's parameters. F is a real and constant factor € [0, 2] which controls the amplification of the differential variation in Equation (4.9).

Step-4: Crossover

The mutated vector's parameters are then mixed with the parameters of another predetermined vector, the target vector, to yield the so called trial vector. Parameter mixing is often referred to as "crossover" which increases the diversity of the perturbed parameter vectors. After generating the donor vector (mutated vector) through mutation, its components are exchanged with target vector which is parent vector from current generation.

Binomial crossover is performed on each of N variable according to crossover probability. The number of parameters inherited from the donor has a binomial distribution. Crossover reinforcing prior successes by generating new vector out of existing object vector parameters. The crossover probability is used to determine that the new vector is to be recombined or not. If the value of the random number is less or equal to the value of the crossover constant, the parameter will come from the mutant vector, otherwise the parameter comes from the parent vector. At the end of crossover, a trial vector is formed in Equation (4.10).

$$K_{mi,G+1} = (K_{1mi,G+1}, K_{2mi,G+1}, \ldots\ldots K_{Nmi,G+1})$$

$$K_{mi,G+1} = \begin{cases} K_{mi,G+1} \; if\,(\text{randb(j)} \leq \text{CR}) \text{ or } \text{j} = rnbr(\text{i}) \\ K_{i,G+1} \; if\,(\text{randb(j)} > \text{CR}) \text{ or } \text{j} \neq \text{rnbr(i)} \end{cases} \quad (4.10)$$

where j=1, 2...NP; rand b(j) is the jth evaluation of a uniform random number generator. CR is the crossover constant € [0, 1]. rnbr (i) is a randomly chosen index € 1,2,.....NP.

Step-5: Selection or Recombination

The new generated vector is obtained by evaluating the fitness function which is an eigen value based multi-objective function with the combination of damping factor and damping ratio. Selection determines whether the target vector is suitable for next iteration or not. To decide whether or not it should become a member of generation G+1, the trial vector K_{mi}, G+1 is compared to the target vector K_i, G using the greedy criterion. If vector K_{mi}, G+1 yields a smaller cost function value than K_i, G, then K_i, G is set to K_{mi}, G+1 ; otherwise, the old value K_i, G is retained. Thus the selection operator chooses the vectors that are going to compose the population in the next generation. This operator compares the fitness of the trial vector and fitness of the corresponding target vector and selects the one that performs better.

Step-6: Stopping Criteria

If the end condition is satisfied, stop and return the best solution in current population.

4.6 SIMULATION RESULTS AND DISCUSSIONS

4.6.1 Hybrid Coordinated controller Design of PSS with SVC, GHC and DSTATCOM Controllers

The coordinated design of PSS, SVC and DSTATCOM controllers is done by applying HCCO algorithm for the minimization of the eigen value based objective function. Here, we have hybrid coordinated designs such as 'PSS+DSTATCOM', 'PSS+GHC' and 'PSS+GHC+DSTATCOM'. The obtained control parameters of controllers in these designs are given in Table 4.2. From these results, one can notice that the real parts of the poorly damped eigen values are shifted to the left side of D-shape curve in the S-plane. For the instance electromechanical modes are shifted from for normal, heavy, light and leading PF conditions respectively with proposed hybrid coordinated controller design.

Table 4.2 HCCO tuned optimal parameter values of proposed (PSS+GHC+DSTATCOM)

Control Parameter	PSS	SVC	DSTATCOM	PROPOSED HCC
K_I	13.2848	1.0586	1.2014	1.5640
T_1	0.3714	0.2540	0.2666	0.2723
T_2	0.3058	0.3879	0.3915	0.4199

To assess the effectiveness and robustness of proposed designed controllers, simulation studies are carried out for six cycle severe fault over a wide range of system load conditions. The electromechanical modes and the damping ratios of test power system with different controller designs under different load conditions are given in Table 4.3. The response curves of the test system under different load conditions are represented in Figures 4.8–4.11, with the proposed coordinated design (PSS + GHC + DSTATCOM). The performance of the HCCO based hybrid coordinated Controller design is quite prominent in comparison to PSS, (PSS + DSTATCOM) and (PSS + GHC + DSTATCOM) controller designs. The overshoots and settling time are significantly improved for the proposed coordinated design.

Table 4.3 Electromechanical modes and ζ under different controllers and load conditions

No control	PSS+DSTATCOM	HCC (PSS+GHC+DSTATCOM)
Normal load		
-0.1615±4.8128i, 0.0335	-1.9441±3.4185i, 0.4944	-3.9249±3.8318i, 0.7155
Heavy load		
-0.1740±4.9589i, 0.0351	-1.9781±3.3800i, 0.5051	-4.2406±3.7515i, 0.7490
Light load		
-0.1521±4.5620i, 0.0333	-1.8873±3.3985i, 0.4855	-3.4832±3.8496i, 0.6709
Leading PF condition		
-0.1975±3.6022i, 0.0547	-1.6246±2.8755i, 0.4919	-3.0910±3.5806i, 0.6535

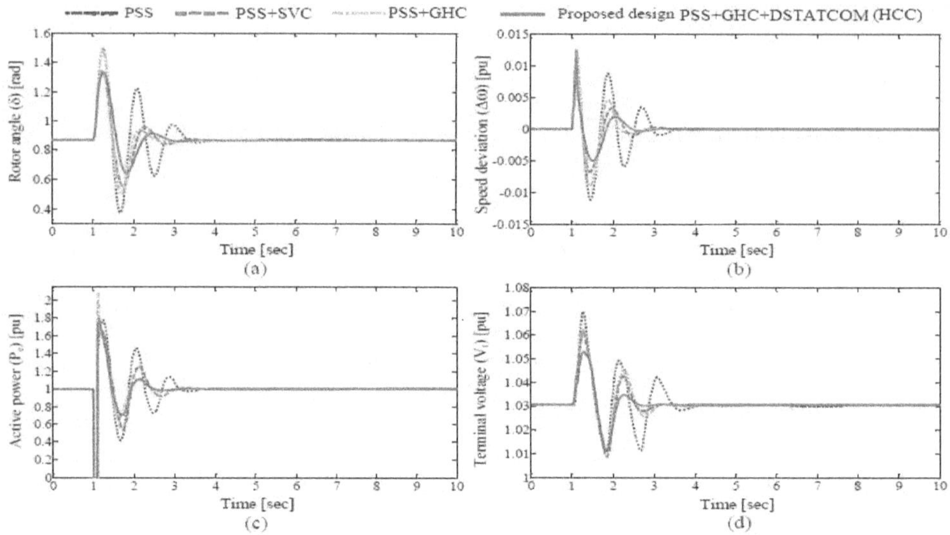

Figure 4.8 Test system dynamic response for a six cycle 3-phase fault under normal load

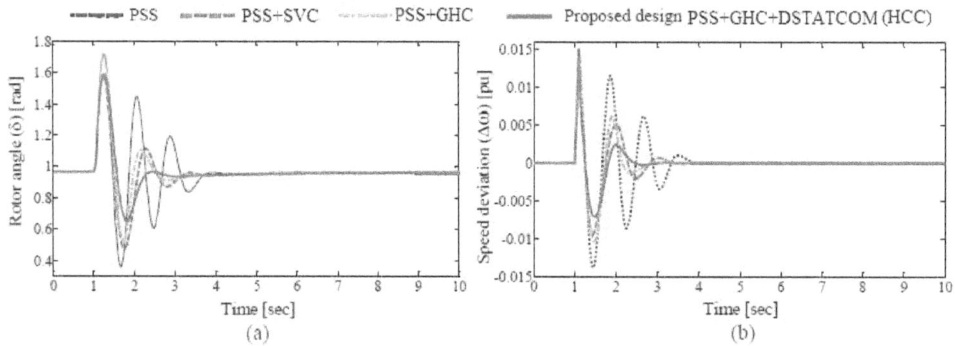

Figure 4.9 Test system dynamic response for a six cycle 3-phase fault under heavy load

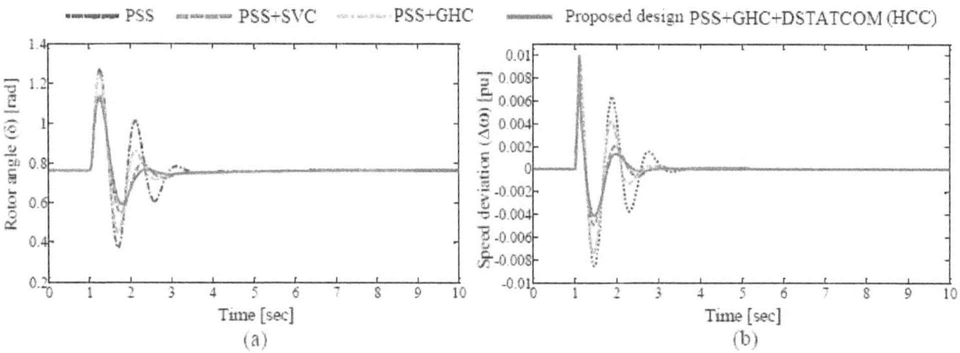

Figure 4.10 Test system dynamic response for a six cycle 3-phase fault under light load

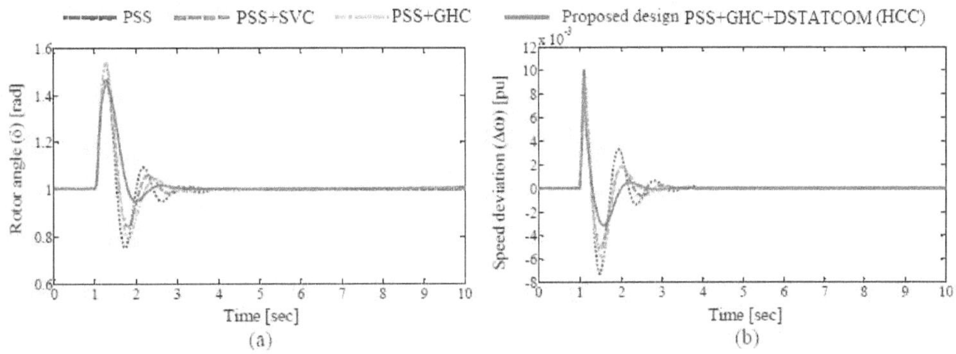

Figure 4.11 Test system dynamic response for a six cycle 3-phase fault under leading PF condition

4.7 SUMMARY

This chapter proposed the algorithm for the hybrid synchronized design of PSS with series and shunt damping controllers. Here, POD based PSS, GHC and DSTATCOM damping controllers are considered for hybrid synchronized design. Two optimised HCC and PID internal controllers are considered for analysis namely for different HCCO. The problem of selecting the damping controller parameter values of different controllers in synchronized design is modelled as optimization problem. Then, the HCCO algorithm is successfully applied to find the optimal solution of the design problem. The effectiveness of proposed synchronized tuned controllers has been tested on a simple test power system through the simulation studies under different loading conditions. The eigen value analysis and nonlinear time domain simulation results show the robustness of proposed controllers and their ability to provide good damping of system oscillations under severe disturbance.

CHAPTER 5

MODELLING OF MULTIMACHINE POWER STABILITY CONTROLLER FOR POWER SYSTEM STABILITY ANALYSIS

5.1 INTRODUCTION

In Chapter 5, the coordinated design procedure of multi-machine system based PSS and different damping controllers using MMPSC algorithm is discussed. The eigen value based objective function is minimized using MMPSC algorithm and the control parameter values of different controllers are obtained at the end of MMPSC algorithm. The proposed hybrid designs are compared with other coordinated designs and compared results are given over a wide range of operating conditions. Although, this chapter exhibits important aspects of multi-machine system, to analyze the inter area issues in real world one has to exercise with multi-machine power system.

Power system stability control is a challenging task in power generation, transmission and distributions based applications and in many fields. MMPSC control can achieve system stabilization within a prescribed time in conventional controller. However, restricted time control can't ensure the system joining inside particular time autonomous on the underlying condition, which makes unlawful application into the useful system if the underlying condition is obscure early. The proposed MMPSC control conquered the issues in existing systems and constrained time dependability controller. Because of this alluring arrangement, MMPSC control reliability has discovered applications in uniform correct differentiator plan for the multi-specialist system. The proposed MMPSC reduces damping oscillation and improve the power system stability control. The main objective of proposed controller is to improve the stability of MMPSC limited time system stabilization independent of the initial state and ensure fast convergence both far away from and at a close range of the power monitoring system. This feature can reduce the loss caused by unwanted oscillation and avoid voltage collapse. To overcome the linearity problem of terminal mode control, saturation function is introduced to limit the amplitude of power input. In comparison with the existing results on stability control, the proposed MMPSC controller applies a simpler method to overcome stability problem and achieves higher efficiency.

5.2 MULTIMACHINE SYSTEM

Control systems unit characterized into three distinct stages specifically era, transmission, and conveyance. In the period unit, the electric power is generally produced by utilizing synchronous generators. Transformers are employed to expand the power and decrease the line streams which naturally diminish the power transmission misfortunes. It is important to keep up the power systems with continuous power supply and voltage solidness. Be that as it may, the capricious occasions, for example, lightning, mishaps or some other necessary circumstance, short circuits between the transmission lines deliver a blame. The above issues in the power system blame create, at least one generators might be extremely exasperates bringing about an irregularity amongst era and request. On the off chance that the disappointment perseveres and not cleared in a predetermined time span, it might cause extreme harms to the hardware which thusly may prompt to a power misfortune and electricity blackout.

From the above discussion, this work proposes a time constrained MMPSC method and applies it to design energy storage device controller for noise reduction in power system. The main advantage of proposed controller is that it can guarantee finite time system stabilization independent on initial state and ensure fast convergence both far away from and at a close range of the control objective. This feature can reduce the loss caused by instant oscillation and avoid voltage collapse. In order to overcome the singularity problem of load voltage control, saturation function is introduced to limit the amplitude of control input. In comparison with the existing results such as AVR and Artificial Neural Network (ANN) on fixed-time control, the proposed controller applies a simpler method to overcome singularity problem and achieves faster convergence.

Hence the proposed work implementation based on closed loop system stability analysis involved in the system models has been presented. The open loop system is unstable, three damping controllers are implemented in the Multi-machine system to enhance the system stability. An itemized steadiness investigation has been introduced, because of the processed eigen values, damping proportions and deviation reactions of the system models. Given the different shut circle stability investigation, it is evident that the proposed MMPSC is better than the Conventional AVR and ANN based controller for Multi-machine power system stability enhancement.

5.3 MULTI-MACHINE POWER SYSTEM COMPENSATION CONTROLLER (MMPSC) METHODOLOGY

The standard control structure plan for voltage reliability model is showed up in Figure 5.1. MMPSC plan is associated with outline MMPSC controller and vitality storing machine controller for energy stability change in power structure. The power system demonstrates of two generator buses and one load bus. One generator bus is managed as a slack bus, while the other generator is furnished with vitality stockpiling gadget, and strength condition can depict its progression. The heap bus incorporates a dynamic acceptance engine in parallel with a consistent PQ stack and an MMPSC. The numerical model for the dominant driving force, MMPSC, and vitality stockpiling gadget controller, are portrayed in the segment of a clear plan.

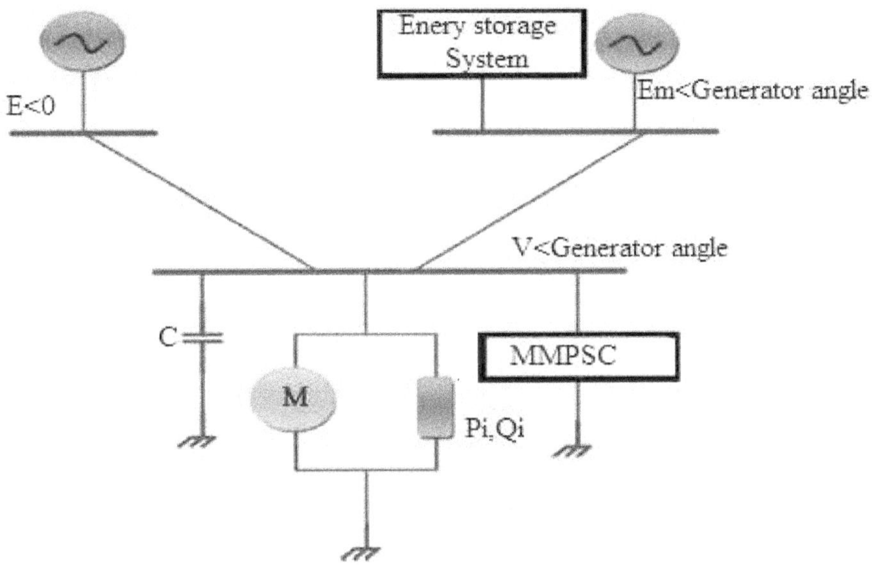

Figure 5.1 Multi-Point Crossover

Multi-machine control remuneration control can accomplish system adjustment inside a recommended time, and it has been connected in many fields. The proposed multi-machine power pay control beats the issues in existing systems and constrained time soundness controller. Because of this appealing arrangement, multi-machine power pays control steadiness has discovered applications in uniform correct differentiator plan for the multi-specialist system. Notwithstanding, multi-machine control remuneration controller proposed a nonlinear time terminal mode controller for a class of second-request nonlinear systems. Be that as it may, the proposed technique wipes out the joining time of the multi-machine controller is provides an optimal solution and also it is used to remove system complications.

5.4 MODELLING OF MMPSC CONTROLLER

The mathematical model for the dynamic motor, MMPSC and energy storage device controller are Taken from looking like conditions. The elements of controlled power system model can be portrayed as: The disparity holds along each trail of the multi-machine control system. The proposed work reconsider the accompanying explanation. Consider a transmission arrange interconnects a multi-machine control system fulfilling suspicion 1 with N generators portrayed by taking after Equations and M loads.

Let $\boldsymbol{\varepsilon}^*$ be an equilibrium point for the generators that is consistent with all the equations describing the power system. The equilibrium $\boldsymbol{\varepsilon}^*$ is globally asymptotically stable if Equation is (5.1).

$$(L_{ss,i} I^*_{x,i})^2 + (L_{ss,i} I^*_{y,i})^2 < 4\ D_i r_i \tag{5.1}$$

holds for all i {f1....... Ng}.

Be that as it may, we can outline a control law, where an MMPSC compensator gadget implements a voltage drop of Equation (5.2), and an MMPSC gadget upholds a present drop off at the terminals of the ith generator in Equation (5.3),

$$T_{\theta i}^{T} - (T_{\theta i}^{T})V_{abc,I}^{*} \tag{5.2}$$

$$T_{\theta i}^{T} - (T_{\theta i}^{T})I_{abc,I}^{*} \tag{5.3}$$

where θ_i is the rotor point of the ith generator, θ_i is the reference rotor edge of a similar generator and T_θ is characterized in Equation (5.4).

$$T_\theta = \frac{\sqrt{2}}{3}\begin{bmatrix} \cos(\theta) & \cos(\theta - \frac{2\pi}{3}) & \cos(\theta + \frac{2\pi}{3}) \\ \sin(\theta) & \sin(\theta - \frac{2\pi}{3}) & \sin(\theta + \frac{2\pi}{3}) \\ \frac{\sqrt{2}}{2} & \frac{\sqrt{2}}{2} & \frac{\sqrt{2}}{2} \end{bmatrix} \tag{5.4}$$

We take note of that $T_\theta^{-1} = T_\theta^T$ Typically, relentless state point contrasts between the generators are given, and the reference rotor edges can be developed from the earlier from this data by picking one of the standard state advantages as the reference outline. Under this control law, the voltages and streams in XYZ organizes at the ith generator terminals get to be

$$V_{xyz,i,new} = V_{xyz,i} - (T_{\theta i}^{T} - T_{\theta i*}^{T})V_{abc,i}^{*} = T_{\theta i}^{T} V_{abc,i} \tag{5.5}$$

$$I_{xyz,i,new} = I_{xyz,i} - (T_{\theta i}^{T} - T_{\theta i*}^{T})I_{abc,i}^{*} = T_{\theta i}^{T} I_{abc,i} \tag{5.6}$$

Conditions (5.5) and (5.6) demonstrates that by applying voltage drop and current drop, we can level the incremental power in XYZ and abc organizes, i.e., Equation (5.7)

$$V^{T}_{xyz,i,new} I_{xyz,i,new} = V^{T}_{abc,i} T_{\theta i} T^{T}_{\theta i} I_{abc,i} = V^{T}_{abc,i} I_{abc} \quad (5.7)$$

We now demonstrate that, under the activity of these controllers, MMPSC is consistently fulfilled.

5.5 DESIGN IMPLEMENTATION OF MMPSC

The fundamental objective of proposed remuneration plan is that the multi-machine ought to have a quick reaction and flexible system. The usage of the draft MMPSC control calculations relies on upon the accompanying strides:

1. Multi-machine system voltages and current estimations
2. Control flag era or regulation
3. Estimation of repaying signs

The control square is appeared in Figure 5.2 utilized which switch unadulterated wave MMPSC modules as required to control the outer gadgets, for example, mechanically exchanged capacitor banks. The extraction of the present segments builds the execution of proposed power calculation. The explanatory consequences of MMPSC controllers furnish quick changing as for the voltage direction yield for each heap conditions. The voltage lists brought on by responsive power worry in the circulation and transmission energy where controlled by proposed MMPSC.

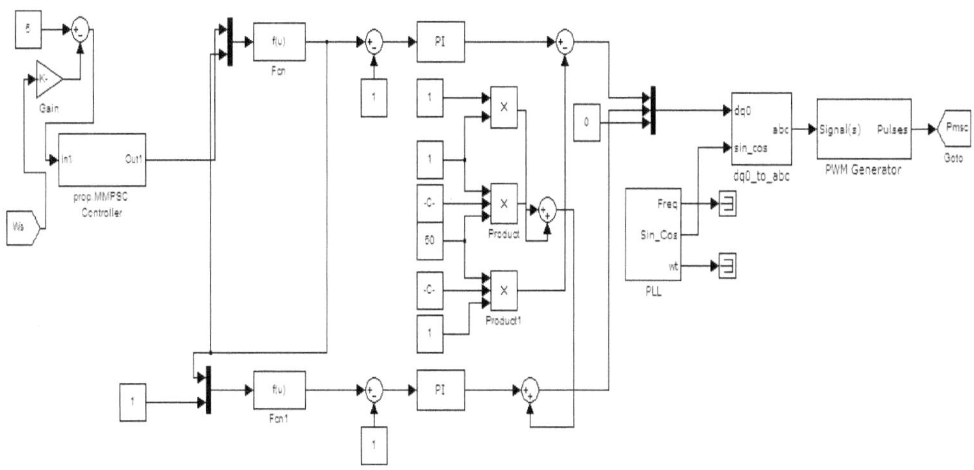

Figure 5.2 Control block of MMPSC

The three-stage different load streams in the a-b-c reference edge can be communicated as taking after the Equations (5.8) and (5.9).

$$\begin{bmatrix} \tilde{V}^{L}_{ab} \\ \tilde{V}^{L}_{bc} \\ \tilde{V}^{L}_{ca} \end{bmatrix} = \begin{bmatrix} 1 & 1 & 1 \\ 1 & \alpha^2 & \alpha \\ 1 & \alpha & \alpha^2 \end{bmatrix} \begin{bmatrix} \tilde{V}^{L}_{u,0} \\ \tilde{V}^{L}_{u,1} \\ \tilde{V}^{L}_{u,2} \end{bmatrix} = [T] \begin{bmatrix} \tilde{V}^{L}_{u,0} \\ \tilde{V}^{L}_{u,1} \\ \tilde{V}^{L}_{u,2} \end{bmatrix} \tag{5.8}$$

$$\begin{bmatrix} \bar{I}^{L}_{a} \\ \bar{I}^{L}_{b} \\ \bar{I}^{L}_{c} \end{bmatrix} = \begin{bmatrix} Y^{L}_{ab} & 0 & -Y^{L}_{ca} \\ -Y^{L}_{ab} & Y^{L}_{bc} & 0 \\ 0 & -Y^{L}_{bc} & Y^{L}_{ca} \end{bmatrix} \begin{bmatrix} \tilde{V}^{L}_{ab} \\ \tilde{V}^{L}_{bc} \\ \tilde{V}^{L}_{ca} \end{bmatrix} \tag{5.9}$$

A spiral dissemination system with an unbalance stack and an MMPSC applying the regular parts strategy exchanges the three-stage stack streams to positive and negative arrangement segments, as appeared, the linnet-line voltages are expected equivalent to rearrange the determination of the remuneration conspire.

$$\bar{I}^{L}_{1} = (1-\alpha) Y^{L}_{0} V^{L}_{u}$$

$$\bar{I}^{L}_{2} = (1-\alpha^2) Y^{L}_{1} V^{L}_{u}$$

Where $\begin{bmatrix} Y_0^L \\ Y_1^L \\ Y_2^L \end{bmatrix} = \frac{1}{3}\begin{bmatrix} 1 & 1 & 1 \\ 1 & \alpha^2 & \alpha \\ 1 & \alpha & \alpha^2 \end{bmatrix}\begin{bmatrix} Y_{ab}^L \\ Y_{bc}^L \\ Y_{ca}^L \end{bmatrix}, V_{ll}^L = |\tilde{V}_{ll,1}^L|$ (5.10)

The discovery of the heap power can be acquired by means of two wattmeter technique, as appeared in Equation (5.10), the positive and negative-arrangement stack streams are spoken to with line-to-line dynamic and responsive forces, as demonstrated Equation (5.11).

$$(\tilde{V}_{ab}^L)^* (\bar{I}_a^L) = (V_{ll}^L \angle -30^o)\,[(\bar{I}_1^L) + (\bar{I}_2^L)]$$

$$(\tilde{V}_{cb}^L)^* (\bar{I}_c^L) = (V_{ll}^L \angle -90^o)\,[\alpha(\bar{I}_1^L) + \alpha^2(\bar{I}_2^L)]$$

$$\begin{bmatrix} \bar{I}_1^L \\ \bar{I}_2^L \end{bmatrix} = \frac{1}{|V_{ll}^L|(\alpha-1)}\begin{bmatrix} 1\angle 150^o & 1\angle 150^o \\ 1\angle -150^o & 1\angle -30^o \end{bmatrix}\begin{bmatrix} P_{ab}^L - jQ_{ab}^L \\ P_{cb}^L - jQ_{cb}^L \end{bmatrix} \quad (5.11)$$

For quick load pay, the MMPSC ought to repay the imaginary part of the positive-succession stack current and the total negative-arrangement stack current in at the earliest opportunity. Along these lines, the power source supplies just genuine part of the positive-grouping load current. Since no zero arrangement segment shows up in the three-stage three-wire system, the remuneration current can be gotten from Equations 5.12 and 5.13. At last, the required pay current of the MMPSC for load compensation is acquired, as appeared

$$\begin{bmatrix} I_a^c \\ I_b^c \\ I_c^c \end{bmatrix} = \begin{bmatrix} \frac{1}{2\sqrt{3}} + j\frac{1}{2} & \frac{-1}{\sqrt{3}} & \frac{1}{2} - j\frac{\sqrt{3}}{2} \\ \frac{-1}{\sqrt{3}} & \frac{1}{2\sqrt{3}} - j\frac{1}{2} & \frac{-1}{2} + j\frac{\sqrt{3}}{2} \\ \frac{1}{2\sqrt{3}} - j\frac{1}{2} & \frac{1}{2\sqrt{3}} + j\frac{1}{2} & 0 \end{bmatrix}\begin{bmatrix} P_{ab}^L / V_{ll}^L \\ P_{cb}^L / V_{ll}^L \\ Q_{ab}^L / V_{ll}^L \end{bmatrix} \quad (5.12)$$

$$\bar{I}_a^c = \mathrm{Im}(\bar{I}_1^L) + \bar{I}_2^L,\ \bar{I}_b^c = \alpha^2 \mathrm{Im}(\bar{I}_1^L) + \alpha\bar{I}_2^L,\ \bar{I}_c^c = \alpha\mathrm{Im}(\bar{I}_1^L) + \alpha^2\bar{I}_2^L \quad (5.13)$$

The general remuneration plan of the MMPSC is presently finished. $|I_r| = K_P \Delta v_{dc} + K_i \int \Delta v_{dc} dt$ (5.14)

For quick continuous pay, the MMPSC needs to distinguish the line-to-line control information rapidly to compute the required pay currently, as Equation in 5.14. With a superior DSP-based system, the remuneration conspires, and other significant capacities in regards to power identifications can be executed rapidly. Along these lines, the need for measuring instruments is lessened. It mutually decreases the building expense of the MMPSC and improves the system consistent quality. Figure 5.3 is the stream diagram of MMPC outline system.

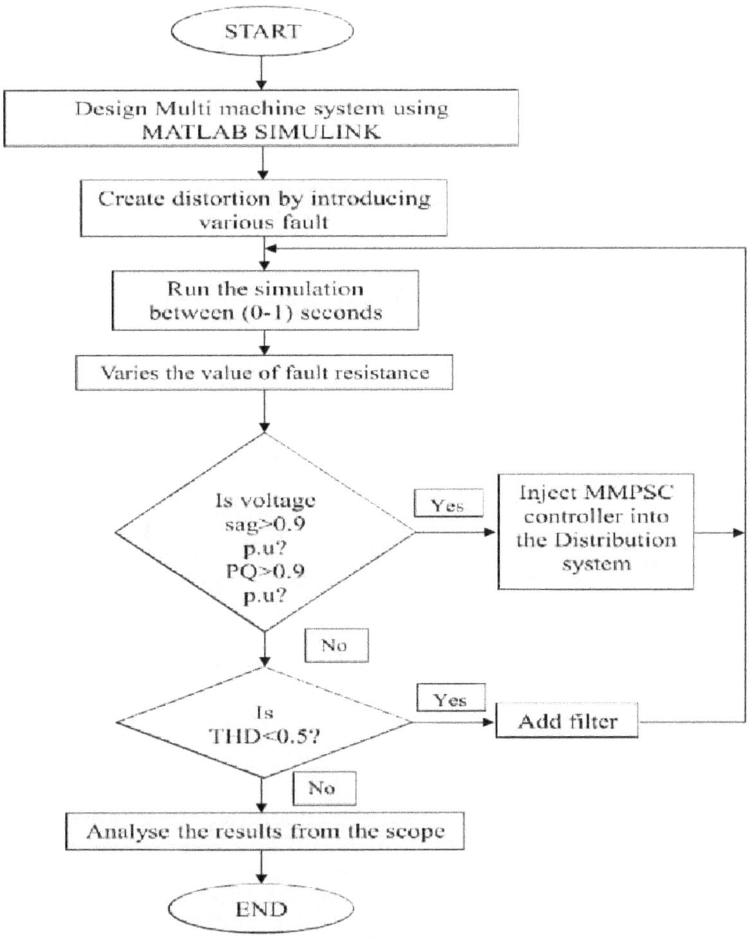

Figure 5.3 Flowchart of MMPSC Design Methodology

5.6 RESULTS AND DISCUSSION

The proposed MMPSC controller have been designed and simulated in Matlab tool, under different fault conditions. Each method has been tested for its voltage stability improvement in number of factors such as frequency, speed deviation, power angle deviation and time duration under scenarios. The simulated test results on IEEE Bus systems show the performance of the MMPSC controller as follows.

5.7 IEEE TEST SYSTEM

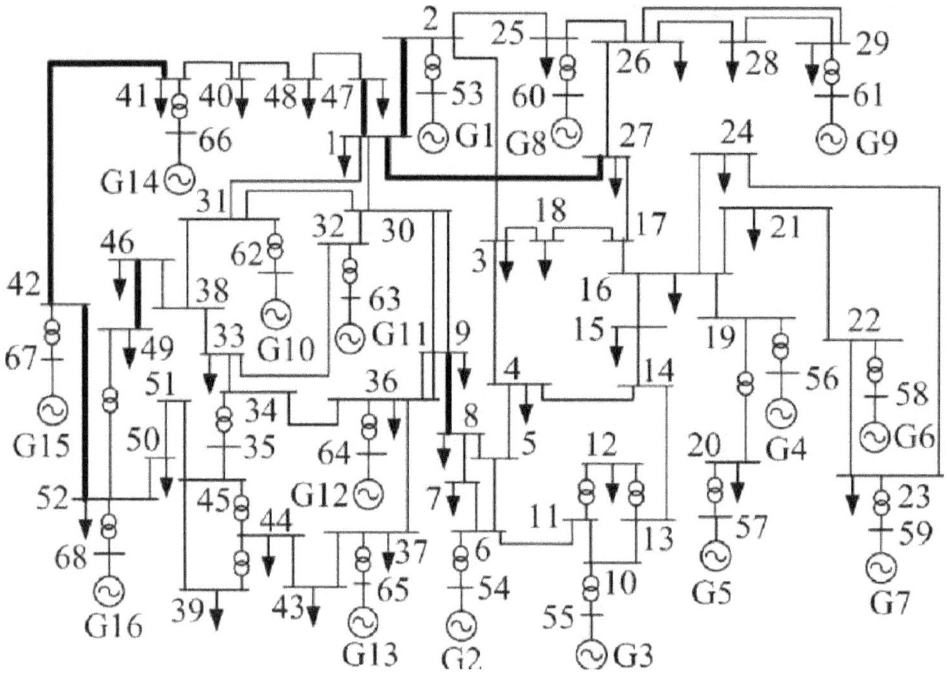

Figure 5.4 Single line diagram of 16-machine 68-bus system

Test system described to implement a two IEEE test systems namely two-area test system and 16-machine, a 68-bus system for identification of inter-area oscillations. The proposed method also validated on real time signals captured by WAFMS at Indian Institute of Technology, Mumbai, India.

A benchmark model consisting of 16-machine, 68-bus system shown in Figure 5.4 represents five geographical regions with tie-lines highlighted by a thick line. This proposed system a reduced order equivalent of the interconnected New England Test System (NETS) and New York Power System (NYPS). The first nine machines represent NETS generation, while represent NYPS generation. The last three machines represent three other neighbouring areas which are approximated by their equivalent generator models. The detailed description of the test system along with network, devices and bus data are available. All machines have static exciters with PSS installed on all machines except for generators 13, 14, 15 and 16. Loads are modelled as constant impedance type. For the present work, tie-lines 46-49 and 1-47 are assumed to be out of commission.

5.8 PARAMETER COLLECTION OF IEEE TEST SYSTEM ANALYSIS

Table 5.1 demonstrates the Evaluation parameters, for example, recurrence and damping proportions of four between zone modes system. The quantity of generators working every mode is additionally given. Therefore the generator angle, frequency deviation and load voltage are depends on the number of generators participation in generation.

Table 5.1 Stability investigation parameters under various method of IEEE 16 bus System

Modes	Frequency(Hz)	Damping value	Contributing Generators
1	0.2199	0.2366	G9,G2-G7,G16G12-G14,
2	0.4382	0.0939	G16,G14
3	0.6613	0.0885	G9,G3-G7,G12,G13
4	0.7727	0.0859	G14,G15,G16

5.9 MULTI-MACHINE SYSTEM OSCILLATIONS DAMPING ANALYSIS

Implementation of the proposed MMPSC controllers in Multi-machine model provides the optimal controller parameters. The MMPSC system damping analysis oscillations in the form of rotor speed and power angle deviations are represented in Figures 5.5 to 5.8 for generators G2 and G3 for various operating conditions and disturbances. The experimental oscillations for all operating conditions in non-linear time domain based MMPSC controller results are as follows.

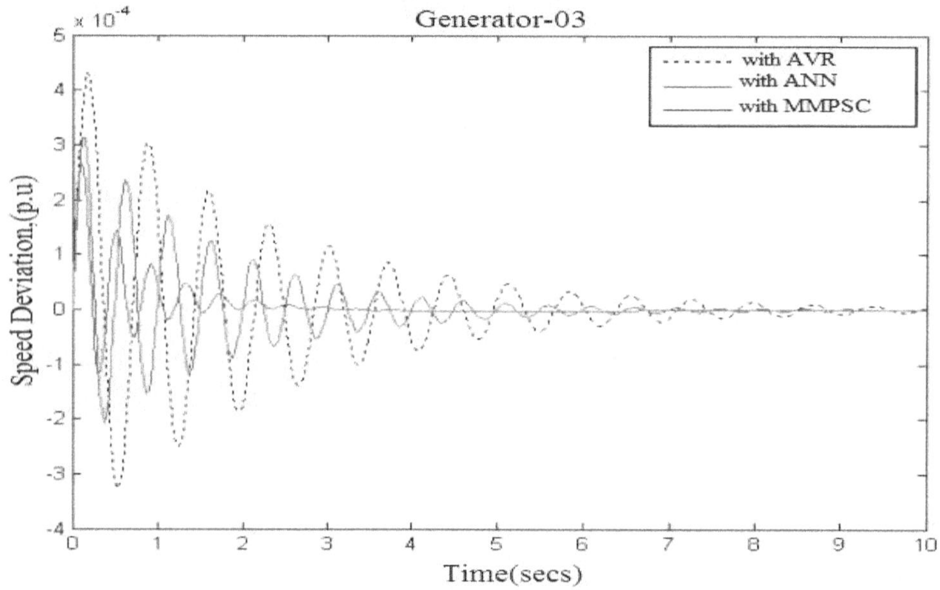

Figure 5.5 Speed deviation responses of G3 for P=0.33, Q=0.03, ΔPd=0.02p.u

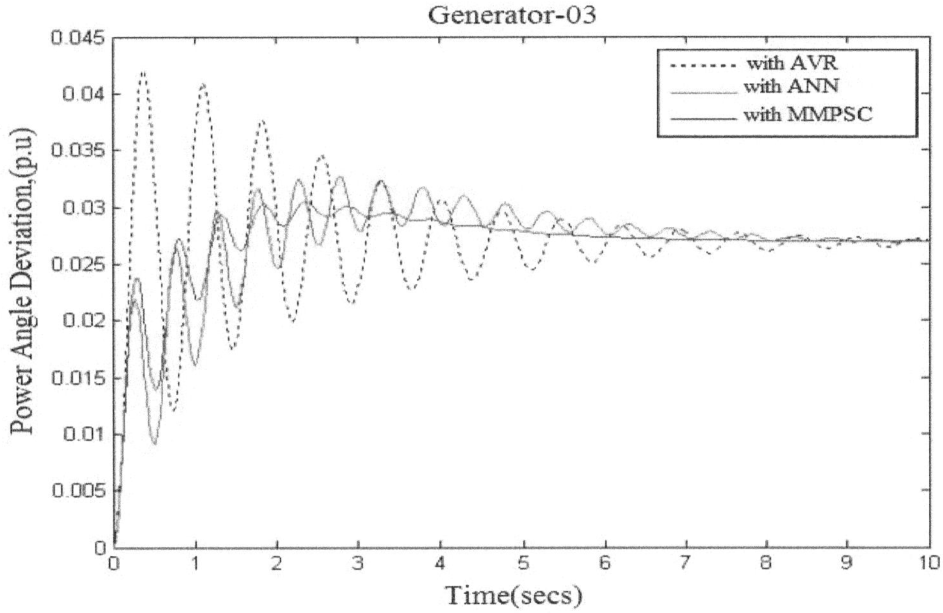

Figure 5.6 Power angle deviation responses of G3 for P=0.24, Q=0.055, ΔPd=0.02p.u condition

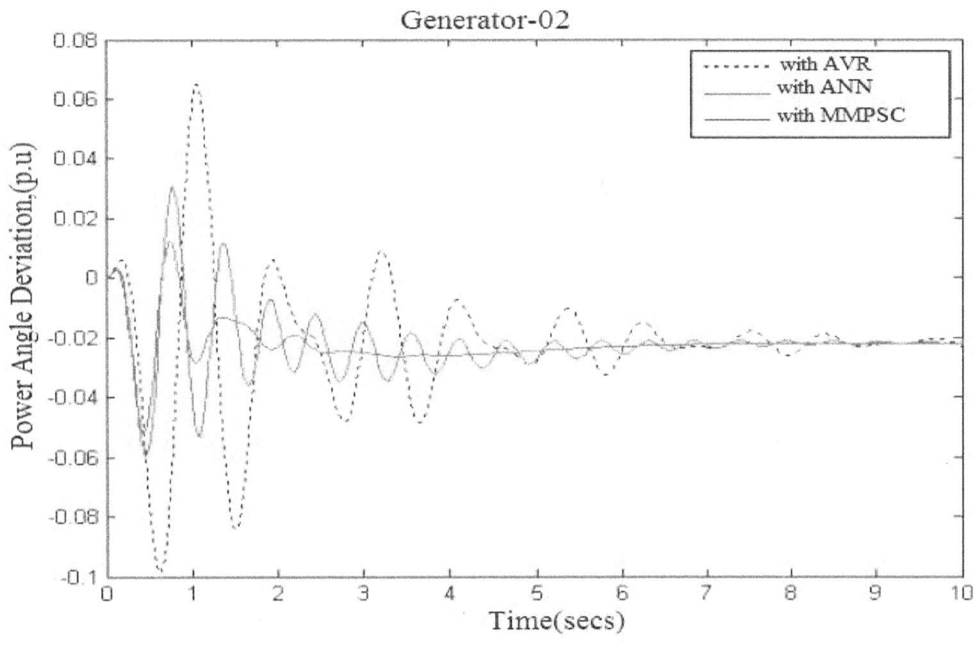

Figure 5.7 Power angle deviation responses of G2 for P=0.61, Q=0.051, ΔPd=0.03p.u condition

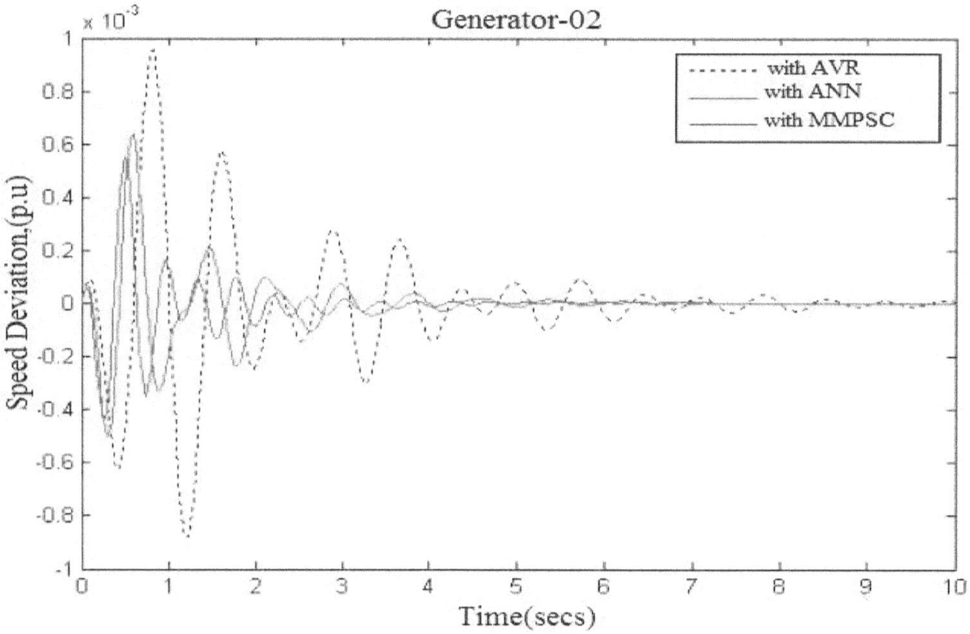

Figure 5.8 Speed deviation responses of G2 for P=0.24, Q=0.055, ΔPd=0.02p.u condition

The above results show the dynamic responses point out the deviation overshoots are minimized and damped as early as possible for the various controllers (AVR, ANN and MMPSC). The better damping oscillation P=0.33, Q=0.03,Pd=0.02p.u., the maximum speed deviation overshoot obtained for AVR is 4.2x10-4p.u, for ANN is $3x10^{-4}$ and for proposed it is $2.6x10^{-4}$p.u.

5.10 COMPARATIVE ANALYSIS OF MMPSC WITH GHC AND HCC CONTROLLERS

The comparison of MPPSC controllers is done by applying MMPSC algorithm for the minimization of the Eigen value based objective function. Here, discussed about the designs such as 'PSS+GHC', 'PSS+HCC' and MMPSC. The obtained control parameters of controllers in these designs are given in Table 5.2. The electromechanical modes and the damping ratios of test power system with different controller designs under different load conditions are given in Table 5.3. From these results, one can notice that the real parts of the poorly damped Eigen values are shifted to the left side of D-shape curve in the S-plane. For the instance electromechanical modes are shifted from for normal, heavy, light and leading PF conditions respectively with proposed MMPSC controller design.

Table 5.2 MMPSC tuned optimal parameter values

Control Parameter	PSS	GHC	HCC	MMPSC
K_I	11.7512	0.9554	1.2014	1.1912
T_1	0.2567	0.2616	0.2666	0.3643
T_2	0.4835	0.2015	0.3915	0.4029

To assess the effectiveness and robustness of proposed designed controllers, simulation studies are carried out for six cycle severe fault over a wide range of system load conditions. The response curves of the test system under different load conditions are represented in Figures 5.9–5.12, with the proposed coordinated design MMPSC. The performance of the MMPSC based controller design is quite prominent in comparison to previous controller designs. The overshoots and settling time are significantly improved for the proposed coordinated design.

Table 5.3 Electromechanical modes and ζ under different controllers and load conditions

No control	GHC	HCC	MMPSC
Normal load			
-0.1615±4.8128i, 0.0335	-1.9441±3.4185i, 0.4944	-3.9249±3.8318i, 0.7155	-3.9322±3.5654i, 0.7408
Heavy load			
-0.1740±4.9589i, 0.0351	-1.9781±3.3800i, 0.5051	-4.2406±3.7515i, 0.7490	-4.2786±3.5095i, 0.7732
Light load			
-0.1521±4.5620i, 0.0333	-1.8873±3.3985i, 0.4855	-3.4832±3.8496i, 0.6709	-3.4470±3.5640i, 0.6952
Leading PF condition			
-0.1975±3.6022i, 0.0547	-1.6246±2.8755i, 0.4919	-3.0910±3.5806i, 0.6535	-3.1303±3.4649i, 0.6704

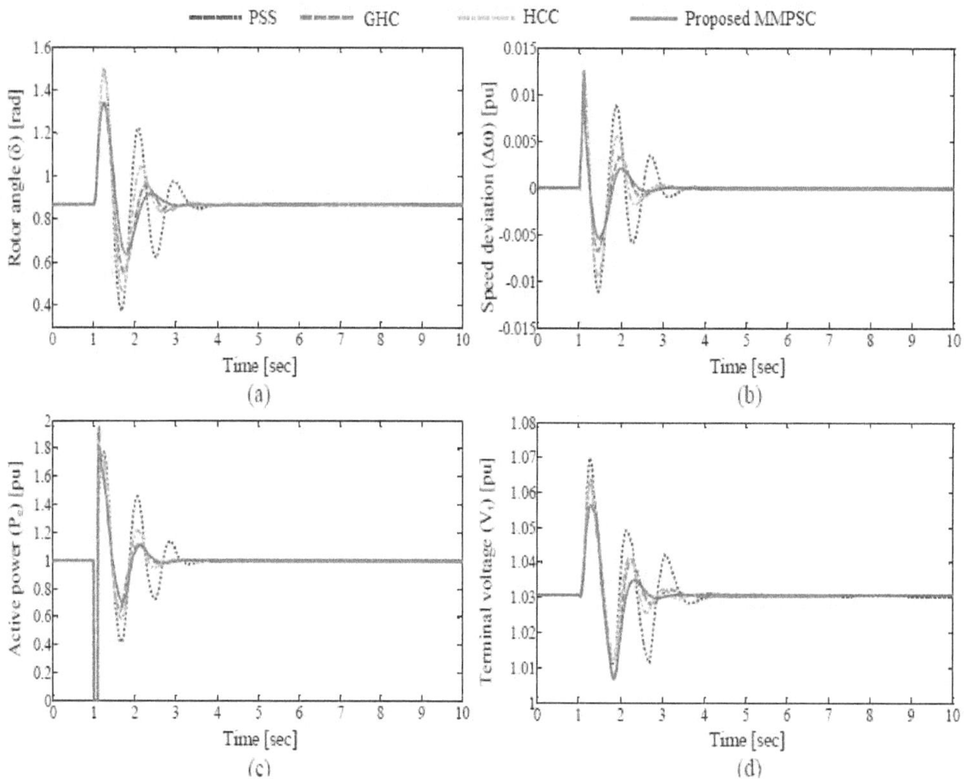

Figure 5.9 Test system dynamic responses for a six cycle 3-phase fault under normal load

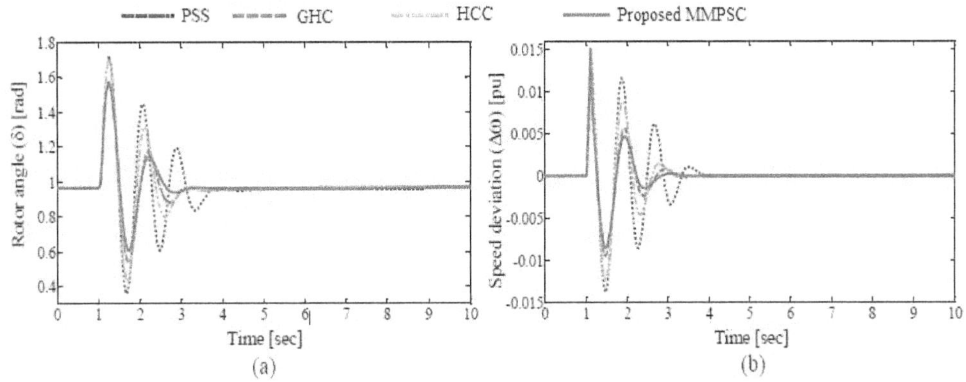

Figure 5.10 Test system dynamic responses for a six cycle 3-phase fault under heavy load

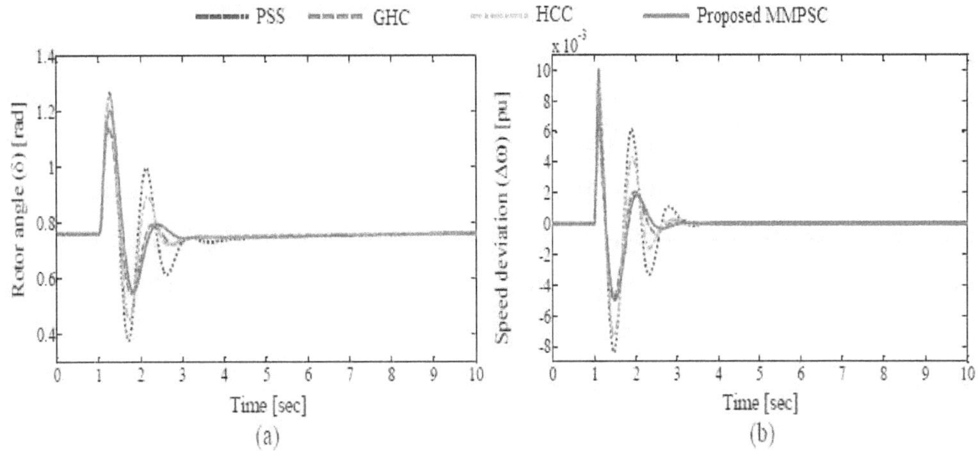

Figure 5.11 Test system dynamic responses for a six cycle 3-phase fault under light load

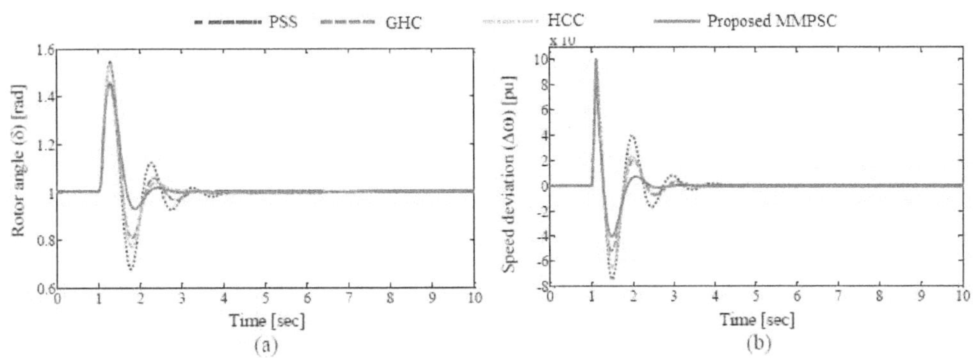

Figure 5.12 Test system dynamic response for a six cycle 3-phase fault under leading PF condition

5.11 SUMMARY

The performances of proposed hybrid coordinated designs are analyzed in multi-machine system environment in this chapter. In this work, two distinct multi-machine test power systems are considered and operated over a wide range of load conditions. The Eigen value analysis and transient stability analysis are done for both the test systems with HCC and MMPSC based coordinated control designs. The proposed hybrid designs provided the integral damping of PSS, series and shunt FACTS controllers together to get best performance. The proposed designs successfully shifted the poorly damped electromechanical mode Eigen values to the left of D-shape curve in *S*-plane. Moreover the damping characteristics of test system with proposed control designs are significantly enhanced in all operating conditions. Furthermore, the settling time comparison of different designs demonstrated that the proposed hybrid designs are far better than the other control designs. In summary, the proposed MMPSC based hybrid coordinated control designs slightly outperforms the proposed HCC based designs.

CHAPTER 6

RESULTS AND DISCUSSION

6.1 INTRODUCTION

The execution of different controller in every one of the components of force stability has been broken down and to enhance the implementation of multimachine steadiness system utilizing various strategies have been proposed. Every plan has considered various controller parameters and several test structures and its strength issues were recognized in every area of the Research. For the problems understood, ideal and proficient arrangements have been proposed, and the controllers have been actualized and recreated utilizing the popular instruments of MATLAB 2013a. In this chapter, a comparative analysis of results is performed for the proposed controller values with the standard PSS. Three different controllers are designed and implemented on different test systems for improving the stability performance of various controllers in the research. Each of the three methods has been implemented and simulated using the MATLAB, and the results havebeen traced and discussed below.

6.2 SIMULATION ENVIRONMENT

All the proposed controller PSS based GHC, HCC, and MMPSC have been implemented in MATLAB with various scenarios. The behaviours of the proposed approaches are analyzed with a variety of simulation parameters. MATLAB is a high-performance language for technical computing. It integrates computation, visualization, and programming in an easy-to-use environment where problems and solutions are expressed in familiar mathematical notation. Typical uses include Sim Power Systems is a modern design tool that allows scientists and engineers to rapidly and easily build models that simulate power systems. Sim Power Systems uses the Simulink environment, allowing you to build a model using simple click and drag procedures. Not only can you draw the circuit topology rapidly, but your analysis of the circuit can include its interactions with mechanical, thermal, control, and other disciplines.

6.3 SIMULATION RESULTS AND ANALYSIS

This section presents the simulation results. A comparison is made with that of the standard previous controller to test and analyze the proposed controllers. A total of two simulations per approach were conducted to evaluate the performance of the proposed approaches by

- Varying the number of test systems
- Varying the load conditions
- Varying the rate of objective function
- Varying the simulation time

The simulation environment is common to all the simulations. The accompanying parameters were embraced to assess performance of the proposed controllers.

- Maximum Peak Overshoot
- Computational Time
- Reduction in the Settling Time

- Critical Clearing Times
- Percentage of stability improvement

6.4 DESCRIPTION OF TEST SYSTEMS

6.4.1 Western System Coordinated Council Test System

Western System Coordinated Council (WSCC) is a three-machine nine-bus system which is shown in Figure 6.1 is documented in (Anderson & Fouad 1977). This is one of the test systems considered for stability analysis that includes three generator and three large equivalent loads connected in a meshed transmission network through transmission lines. The generators are dynamically modelled with the classical equivalent model. IEEE standard excitation, neglecting the saturation of the exciter is considered for each generator model. Otherwise, these machines can be equipped with simple commonly used Type-AC8B AVR. The machine in each area is not equipped with PSS. The dynamics of the system are described by a set of nonlinear differential equations. For the purpose of controller design these equations are linearized around the nominal operating conditions. Figure 6.1 shows the diagrammatic representation of WSCC test system.

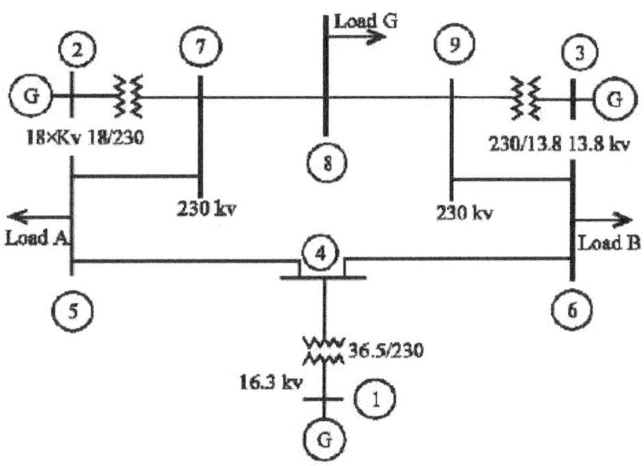

(Source: Anderson & Fouad 1977)

Figure 6.1 WSCC Test Systems

6.4.2 Two-area Test System (TATS)

Two-area Test System (TATS) is an asymmetrical four-machine eight-bus power system. The dynamic equivalent of that realistic power system is as shown in Figure 6.2. The system is clearly split into two-areas, one comprising generators 1 and 2 and the other comprising generators 3 and4. The generators are rated at 900 MVA and 20 kV, with connection to the network through a 20/230 kV step-up transformer. The nominal system is operating with Area 1 exporting 400 MW to Area 2.The electrical loads 967 MW and 1767 MW from the system are static loads and supplies equal active power (Kashki et al. 2010). Load 1 can be varied in the range [1140 to 1540] MW while Load 2 can be varied in the range [1400 to 1800] MW. Results of the initially performed modal analysis (Gegov 1996) identified three electromechanical modes in the system, which include two local oscillatory modes (between generators 1 and 4 between generators 2 and 3, respectively) and an inter-area mode (generators 1 and 4 oscillating against generators 2 and 3). It is assumed that all the four generators are provided with static excitation systems. IEEE type ST1 model of the static excitation system is used. The generators 1 and 2 are located in area 1 while the generators 3 and 4 are located in area 2.

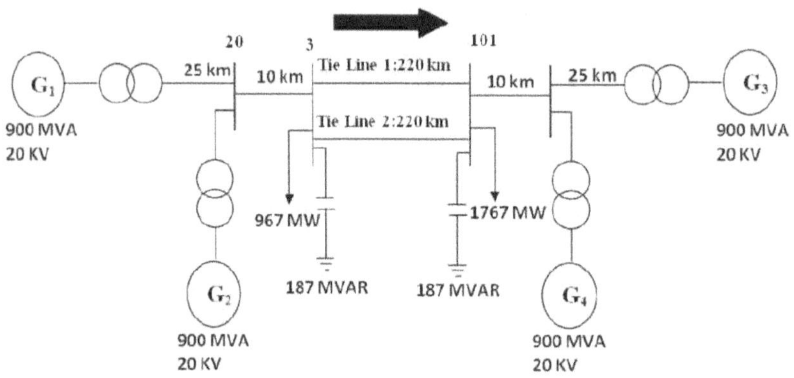

(Source: Mishra et al. 2006)

Figure 6.2 Two-Area Test System

The corresponding dynamic model consists of generators, governors, static exciters, PSS and non-linear voltage and frequency dependent loads. Although a simple network, it has very interesting dynamic sand provides an example for the assessment of AVR or PSS performance. This power network is specifically designed to study low frequency electromechanical oscillations in large interconnected power systems. Despite the small size of this power network, it mimics very closely the behaviour of typical systems in actual operation (Klein et al 1991). It is specifically designed to study low frequency electromechanical oscillations in large inter connected power systems.

6.4.3 New England Test System (NETS)

New England Test System (NETS) is a 39-bus standard for testing new methods. It represents a greatly reduced model of the power system in New England. This IEEE 39-bus system is well known as 10-machine New-England Power System. Synchronous machines are modelled by two – axis model. Generator 1 represents the aggregation of a large number of generators. It has been used by numerous researchers to study both static and dynamic problems in power systems. The 39-bus system has 10 generators, 19 loads, 36 transmission lines and 12 transformers. The 39-bus system is organized into 3 areas. Area 3 contains two portions of the network which are not directly connected. This 10M39B (10 Machine 39 bus system) system documented in Mishra et al. (2007) is a widely recognized New England test system, used in many different studies in the past. Figure 6.3 shows the one line diagram of New England Test System.

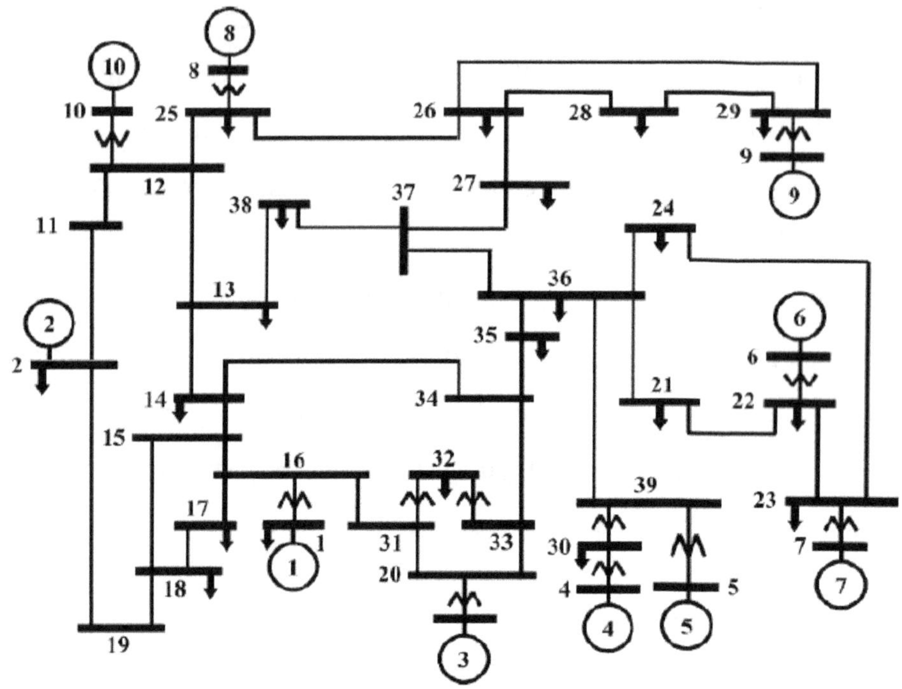

(Source: Martins & Lima 1989)

Figure 6.3 New England Test System

6.4.4 South/Southeast Brazilian Test System

The next well-known system is the seven bus five-machine equivalent of the unstable South/South eastern Brazilian system (SBTS) as pictured in Figure 6.4. The study system is a slightly modified 7-busequivalent of the model used in the initial planning studies of the Itaipu generation and AC transmission complex. The Itaipu generator is connected to the Southeast region (represented by a static load together with a large synchronous motor) through a series compensated 765 KV bus.

An intermediate765 KV bus is connected to a 500 KV transmission ring containing three other hydro stations - S. Santiago, S. Segredo and Fozdo Areia. The AVR models used in the original system were disregarded in favour of a simpler first-order model which is common to all machines. All loads are of the constant impedance type. System data is taken from Martins & Lima (1989).

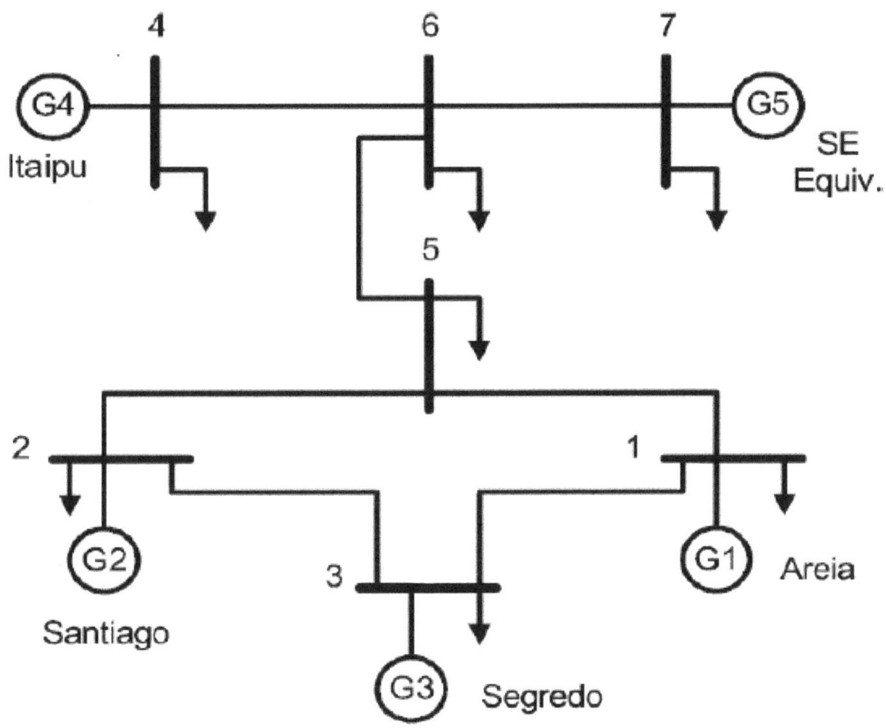

(Source: Martins & Lima 1989)

Figure 6.4 South/Southeast Brazilian Test System

The model analysis of the small Brazilian test system indicates that there are two inter area modes. Mode 1 is due to the Southeast (SE) equivalent system oscillating against the Itaipu generator, Mode 2 is due to the South system (represented by Santiago, Segredo and Areia) oscillating against the Southeast system together with the Itaipu generator. The system also has two local modes of oscillations within the south system: Mode 3 consisting of Areia and Segredo oscillating against Santiago, and Mode 4 consisting of Areia oscillating against Segredo.

6.5 TESTING OF POWER SYSTEM STABILITY PARAMETERS FOR VARIOUS TESTSYSTEMS

In this research work, the following controllers' techniques, Conventional PID (CPID), Standard AVR controller, Conventional Genetic Algorithm based controller (CGA), Proposed GHC, Proposed HCC and MMPSC are applied to design the PSS. In order to demonstrate the effectiveness and robustness of the proposed techniques, several cases with different objectives to minimize the overshoots, reduction in the settling time and power stability enhancement have been considered in PSS design. In this section the results are compared with that of other proposed approaches.

6.5.1 Comparison of Minimization of the Overshoot

Table 6.1 displays the maximum peak overshoot and computational times for WSCC test system by the proposed approaches. An important observation is that the MMPSC obtains better reduction in maximum peak overshoot than other methods. Under heavy loading conditions AVR obtains 0.9% reduction in maximum overshoot, CGA obtains 3.38% reduction in maximum overshoot and GHC obtains 2.02% reduction in maximum overshoot, HCC obtains 5.23% reduction in maximum overshoot, MMPSC obtains 6.13% reduction in maximum overshoot from that of PID. Though, GA and its variants obtain solution in lesser time, their solutions are not better than that of MMPSC. Among HCC and MMPSC, the performance of MMPSC is better than HCC in terms of solution quality and computational time. The computational time for MMPSC is 2 seconds lesser than that of HCC.

Table 6.1 Maximum Peak Overshoot and Computational Time for WSCC Test System

Method	Over Shoot $M_p(x10^3)$		Computational Time in Sec. (T_C)
	Light Loading	Heavy Loading	
PID	8.345	4.911	65
AVR	8.166	4.567	45
CGA	8.258	4.745	36
GHC	7.889	4.812	34
HCC	7.781	4.654	30
MMPSC	7.689	4.61	28

Table 6.2 displays the maximum peak overshoot and computational times for two-area test system by the proposed approaches.

Table 6.2 Maximum Peak Overshoot and Computational Time for TATS

Method	Over Shoot $M_p(x10^3)$		Computational Time in Sec. (T_C)
	Light Loading	Heavy Loading	
PID	8.324	5.2	98
AVR	7.966	4.463	85
CGA	8.058	4.657	76
GHC	7.657	4.454	72
HCC	7.534	4.345	70
MMPSC	7.423	4.271	62

MMPSC obtains better reduction in maximum peak overshoot than other methods. Under heavy loading conditions AVR obtains 14.2% reduction in maximum overshoot, CGA obtains 10.44% reduction in maximum overshoot and GHC obtains 14.35% reduction in maximum overshoot, HCC obtains 16.44% reduction in maximum overshoot, MMPSC obtains 17.87% reduction in maximum overshoot from that of PID. Though, GA and its variants obtain solution in lesser time, their solutions are not better than that of MMPSC. Among HCC and MMPSC, the performance of MMPSC is better than HCC in terms of solution quality and computational time. The computational time for MMPSC is 8 seconds lesser than that of HCC.

Table 6.3 displays the maximum peak overshoot and computational times for New England test system by the proposed approaches.

Table 6.3 Maximum Peak Overshoot and Computational Time for NETS

Method	Over Shoot $M_p(x10^3)$		Computational Time in Sec. (T_C)
	Light Loading	Heavy Loading	
PID	8.453	4.812	112
AVR	8.216	4.322	108
CGA	8.425	4.456	94
GHC	7.289	4.233	92
HCC	7.181	4.012	88
MMPSC	6.889	3.992	78

MMPSC obtains better reduction in maximum peak overshoot than other methods. Under heavy loading conditions AVR obtains 10.18% reduction in maximum overshoot, CGA obtains 7.4% reduction in maximum overshoot and GHC obtains 12.03% reduction in maximum overshoot, HCC obtains 16.63% reduction in maximum overshoot, MMPSC obtains 17.04% reduction in maximum overshoot from that of PID. Though, GA and its variants obtain solution in lesser time, their solutions are not better than that of MMPSC. Among HCC and MMPSC, the performance of MMPSC is better than HCC in terms of solution quality and computational time. The computational time for MMPSC is 10 seconds lesser than that of HCC.

Table 6.4 displays the maximum peak overshoot and computational times for South/Southeast Brazilian test system by the proposed approaches.

Table 6.4 Maximum Peak Overshoot and Computational Time for SBTS

Method	Over Shoot $M_p(x10^3)$		Computational Time in Sec. (T_C)
	Light Loading	Heavy Loading	
PID	7.981	4.712	86
AVR	7.345	3.543	76
CGA	7.876	3.648	64
GHC	7.234	3.321	62
HCC	7.099	3.123	58
MMPSC	6.654	3.012	46

MMPSC obtains better reduction in maximum peak overshoot than other methods. Under heavy loading conditions AVR obtains 24.81% reduction in maximum overshoot, CGA obtains 22.58% reduction in maximum overshoot and GHC obtains 29.52% reduction in maximum overshoot, HCC obtains 33.72% reduction in maximum overshoot, MMPSC obtains 36.08% reduction in maximum overshoot from that of PID. Though, GA and its variants obtain solution in lesser time, their solutions are not better than that of MMPSC. Among HCC and MMPSC, the performance of MMPSC is better than HCC in terms of solution quality and computational time. The computational time for MMPSC is 12 seconds lesser than that of HCC.

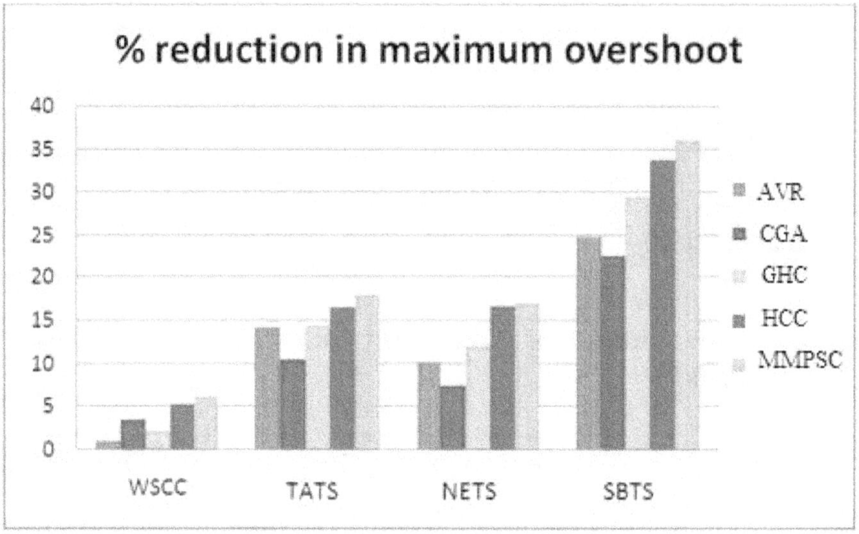

Figure 6.5 Comparison for % reduction in maximum overshoot

6.5.2 Comparison of Reduction in the Settling Time

Table 6.5 displays settling time details of WSCC test system obtained by the proposed methods.

Table 6.5 Settling time for WSCC test system

Method	Settling Time T_c(Sec.)		Success Rate (S_R)
	Light Loading	Heavy Loading	
PID	2.95	2.6	NA
AVR	1.65	1.24	78
CGA	2.75	2.33	79
GHC	1.32	1.16	80
HCC	1.24	1.02	81
MMPSC	1.01	0.91	84

MMPSC reduces the settling time greatly than other methods. Under heavy loading conditions MMPSC has an improvement by 65%, 26.61%, 60.94%, 21.55%, and 10.78% in reducing the settling time as that of PID, AVR, CGA, GHC and HCC respectively for heavy loading conditions.

Table 6.6 displays settling time details of two-area test system obtained by the proposed methods.

Table 6.6 Settling time for TATS

Method	Settling Time T_c(Sec.)		Success Rate (S_R)
	Light Loading	Heavy Loading	
PID	3.12	3.5	NA
AVR	1.55	1.34	83
CGA	2.63	1.83	84
GHC	1.42	1.28	87
HCC	1.34	1.24	90
MMPSC	1.21	1.1	92

It can be seen that, MMPSC reduces the settling time greatly than other methods. MMPSC has an improvement by 68.57%, 17.91%, 39.89%, 14.06% and 11.29% in reducing the settling time as that of PID, AVR, CGA, GHC and HCC respectively for heavy loading conditions.

Table 6.7 displays settling time details of NETS obtained by the proposed methods.

Table 6.7 Settling time for NETS

Method	Settling Time T_c(Sec.)		Success Rate (S_R)
	Light Loading	Heavy Loading	
PID	3.41	2.8	NA
AVR	1.16	1.31	76
CGA	3.36	2.33	77
GHC	1.23	1.23	79
HCC	0.91	1.12	81
MMPSC	0.67	0.89	86

It can be seen that, MMPSC reduces the settling time greatly than other methods. MMPSC has an improvement by 68.21%, 32.06%, 61.8%, 27.64% and 20.54% in reducing the settling time as that of PID, AVR, CGA, GHC and HCC respectively for heavy loading conditions.

Table 6.8 displays settling time details of South/Southeast Brazilian system obtained by the proposed methods.

Table 6.8 Settling time for SBTS

Method	Settling Time T_c(Sec.)		Success Rate (S_R)
	Light Loading	Heavy Loading	
PID	2.95	2.6	NA
AVR	1.65	1.24	78
CGA	2.75	2.33	79
GHC	1.32	1.16	80
HCC	1.24	1.02	81
MMPSC	1.01	0.91	84

MMPSC reduces the settling time greatly than other methods. MMPSC has an improvement by 62.17%, 28.1%, 60.99%, 34.59% and 14.71% in reducing the settling time as that of PID, AVR, CGA, GHC and HCC respectively for heavy loading conditions.

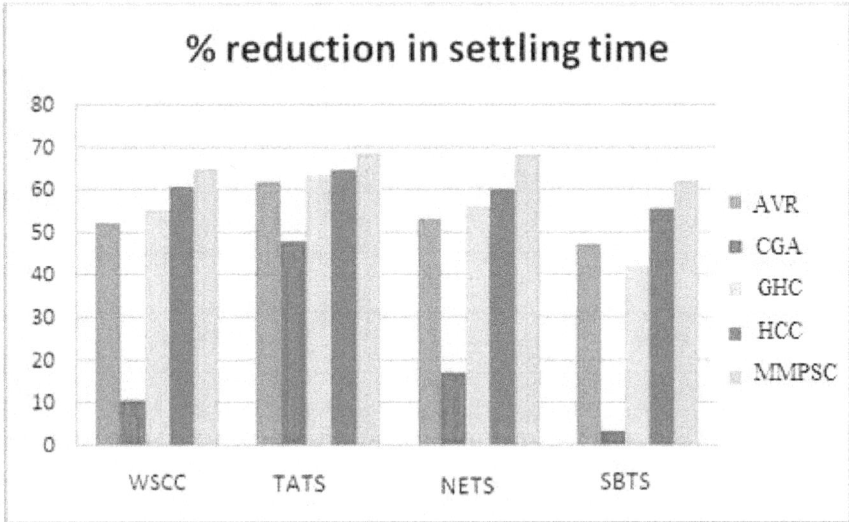

Figure 6.6 Comparison for % reduction in settling time

6.5.3 Correlation of Power System Stability Improvement

A three stage blame for 100ms length is connected to a predetermined bus, trailed by the stumbling of the lines. Under these cases, the central clearing times (in ms) for the proposed methodologies are arranged in Table 6.9 by explaining the swing condition. Given the CCT values, the change in the rate of force system solidness is classified.

Table 6.10 showcases the speed of change in power system stability concerning PID for all test systems by the proposed approaches under various defective conditions.

Table 6.9 Comparison of Critical Clearing Times (100 ms) for Different Approaches

Method	WSCC	TATS	NETS	SBTS
	Faulty Bus-7	**Faulty Tie Line-1**	**Faulty Bus-29**	**Faulty Bus-5**
PID	83	74	83	72
AVR	92	83	92	80
CGA	90	81	90	78
GHC	91	83	92	79
HCC	92	84	91	81
MMPSC	94	86	94	84

Table 6.10 Percentage of power system stability improvement

Method	Improvement %			
	WSCC	TATS	NETS	SBTS
AVR	10. 85	12.16	10. 85	11.11
CGA	9.64	9. 46	8.44	8.11
GHC	13.25	12.16	10. 85	9.72
HCC	14.46	13. 51	9. 64	12. 5
MMPSC	**16. 87**	**16. 22**	**13. 25**	**16.67**

It can be seen that MMPSC based PSS enhances the power system strength enormously than different techniques. For correlation reason the overall execution records of various test system connected with the shut – circle recurrence are given in Table 6.10 under same aggravations.

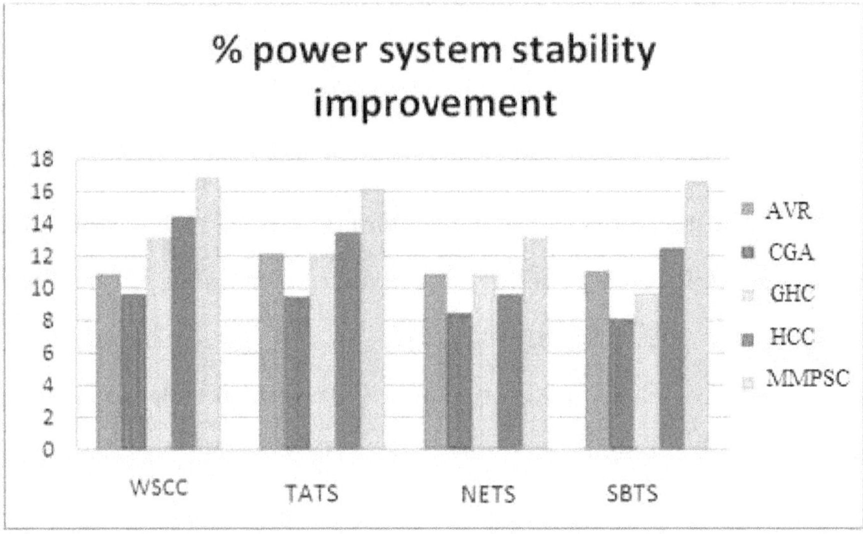

Figure 6.7 Comparison for % Power System Stability Improvement

From Table 6.11 it is clear that the Performance indices are generally accepted values and characterizes the system as a very good damping system. Finally, it is clear that the application of MMPSC based PSS can certainly enhance the overall damping characteristics of the system.

Table 6.11 Performance indices of different test system

Method	WSCC Test System			TATS			NETS			SBTS		
	M_P ($\times 10^{-3}$)	T_s	Sr/Tc	M_P ($\times 10^{-3}$)	T_s	Sr/Tc	M_P ($\times 10^{-3}$)	T_s	Sr/Tc	M_P ($\times 10^{-3}$)	T_s	Sr/Tc
AVR	4.9	2.6	NA/65	5.2	3.5	NA/98	4.8	2.8	NA/112	4.7	2.3	NA/86
CGA	4.86	1.24	78/45	4.46	1.34	83/85	4.32	1.31	76/108	3.54	1.21	78/76
GHC	4.81	1.16	80/34	4.45	1.28	87/72	4.23	1.23	79/92	3.32	1.33	80/62
HCC	4.65	1.02	81/30	4.34	1.24	90/70	4.01	1.12	81/88	3.12	1.02	82/58
MMPSC	**4.61**	**0.91**	**84/28**	**4.27**	**1.1**	**92/62**	**3.99**	**0.89**	**86/78**	**3.01**	**0.87**	**89/46**

Time domain simulations for a set of test cases were carried out to evaluate the performance of the proposed PSS. For a WSCC test system AVR based PSS obtains 4% reduction in maximum overshoot, GHC based PSS obtains 9% reduction in maximum overshoot, QBGA based PSS obtains 25% reduction in maximum overshoot, and **MMPSC based PSS obtains 29% reduction in maximum overshoot** with reference to the maximum overshoot of PID.

From the settling time particulars of WSCC test system it can be seen that, for AVR based PSS there is a reduction in Ts by 52.3%, for GHC based there is a reduction in Ts by 55.4%, for QBGA based there is a reduction in Ts by 60.8%, and **for MMPSC based there is a reduction in Ts by 65%** with reference to the PID design. Simulation of all the multi-machine system shows that the computational time required for simulation is less (**average of 40%**) when compared to the other methods. Thus the implementation and evaluation of MMPSC technique in PSS design is better in terms of solution quality and computational time.

For further comparison, the percentage reductions in maximum overshoot, settling time and power system stability enhancement has been charted in bar diagrams. Figures 6.5 to 6.7 indicate that the performance of MMPSC is better when compared to the other proposed approaches.

6.6 SUMMARY

The need for MMPSC and the implementation of MMPSC in PSS design is presented. Besides, the comparative performances of optimization algorithms for finding the optimal parameters of power system stabilizers in a multi-machine have been presented. The performance of MMPSC is evaluated on two standard test systems and its performance is compared with that of proposed and existing methods reported in the literature. From the performance study, it is found that the performance of MMPSC based PSS is better than that of other methods in terms of computational complexity, success rate and solution quality .It is also established that MMPSC can be applied to solve PSS problem efficiently.

CHAPTER 7

CONCLUSION OF THE RESEARCH AND FUTURE WORK

7.1 CONCLUSION

The execution of various controller in each one of the parts of drive soundness has been dismembered and to upgrade the performance of a multi machine quality system using unique methods of insight have been proposed. Each technique has considered various controller parameters and particular test systems and its soundness issues were perceived at each section of the examination. For the problems seen, whole and viable courses of action have been proposed, and the controllers have been executed and impersonated using the unmistakable instruments of MATLAB 2013.

The first research work mainly focused on DFIG based wind generation system. When integrating a wind farm into the grid one of the major issues that needs to be considered is the power system stability. By considering power system stability as the major challenge, this thesis developed a set of power system stability controller optimization and investigated the impact of the designed PSS's on the grid integrated DFIG based wind generation system. From the investigated results it is observed that the designed power system stabilizers provide a better performance to supply a stable power to the grid. Then, the GHCO algorithm is successfully applied to find the optimal solution of the design problem. The effectiveness of proposed tuned controllers has been tested on a simple test power system through the simulation studies under different loading conditions. The Eigen value analysis and nonlinear time domain simulation results show the robustness of proposed controllers and their ability to provide good damping of system oscillations under severe disturbance.

The second approach proposed the algorithm for the hybrid synchronized design of PSS with series and shunt damping controllers. Here, POD based PSS, GHC and DSTATCOM damping controllers are considered for hybrid synchronized design. Two optimised HCC and PID internal controllers are considered for analysis namely for different HCCO. The problem of selecting the damping controller parameter values of different controllers in synchronized design is modelled as optimization problem. Then, the HCCO algorithm is successfully applied to find the optimal solution of the design problem. The effectiveness of proposed synchronized tuned controllers has been tested on a simple test power system through the simulation studies under different loading conditions. The Eigen value analysis and nonlinear time domain simulation results show the robustness of proposed controllers and their ability to provide good damping of system oscillations under severe disturbance.

The third solution considers, the performances of proposed hybrid coordinated designs are analyzed in multi-machine system environment in this chapter. In this work, two distinct multi-machine test power systems are considered and operated over a wide range of load conditions. The eigen value analysis and transient stability analysis are done for both the test systems with HCC and MMPSC based coordinated control designs. The proposed hybrid designs provided the integral damping of PSS, series and shunt FACTS controllers together to get best performance. The proposed designs successfully shifted the poorly damped electromechanical mode Eigen values to the left of D-shape curve in *S*-plane. Moreover the damping characteristics of test system with proposed control designs are significantly enhanced in all operating conditions.

Furthermore, the settling time comparison of different designs demonstrated that the proposed hybrid designs are far better than the other control designs. In summary, the proposed MMPSC based hybrid coordinated control designs slightly outperforms the proposed HCC based designs.

From the above discussion, it is concluded that each approach has considered various factors of PSS. The final method MMPSC based algorithm produces efficient results.The need for MMPSC and the implementation of MMPSC in PSS design is presented. Besides, the comparative performances of optimization algorithms for finding the optimal parameters of power system stabilizers in a multi-machine have been presented. The performance of MMPSC is evaluated on two standard test systems and its performance is compared with that of proposed and existing methods reported in the literature. From the performance study, it is found that the performance of MMPSC based PSS is better than that of other methods in terms of computational complexity, success rate and solution quality .It is also established that MMPSC can be applied to solve PSS problem efficiently.

7.2 FUTURE WORK

This exploration has investigated some quick thoughts and flexible arrangements. In light of the experience picked up from this work, the accompanying viewpoints require for further examination.

- For future work, the proposed technique can be enhanced by utilizing a superior advancement and seeking strategy under various stack conditions and extremely irritated machines.

- In future, the proposed approach can be improved to be used for operational choices at which quick options are required.

- The strength of proposed plans can be tried by implementing in great power systems (like, 10-machine 39- bus New England control system, 16-machine 68-bus NYPS-NETS test control system).

- Moreover, half and half improvement strategies and progressed control Methods can be utilized as a part of future for ideal tuning of various controllers in Multi-machine systems.

- Prospects ought to be concentrate on the usage of proposed outlines in useful power system applications.

REFERENCES

1. Abbas, HA, Sarker, R & Newton, C 2001, 'PDE: A Pareto-Frontier Differential Evolution Approach for Multi-objective Optimization Problems', Proceedings of the Congress on Evolutionary Computation, vol. 2, pp. 971-978.

2. Abdel Magid, YL Abido, MA, AI-Baiyat, S & Mantawy, AH 1999, 'Simultaneous stabilization of multi machine power systems via genetic algorithms', IEEE Trans. on Power Systems, vol. 14, pp. 1428-1439.

3. Abdel-Magid, YL & Abido, MA 2003, 'Optimal multi objective design of robust power system stabilizers using genetic algorithms', IEEE Trans. on Power Systems, vol. 18, no. 3, pp. 1125-1132.

4. Abdulai, JD, Ould-Khaoua, M & Mackenzie, LM 2009, 'Adjusted Probabilistic route discovery in mobile ad hoc networks', Elsevier, Computers and Electrical Engineering, vol. 35, no. 1, pp. 168-182.

5. Abido, MA 2002, 'Optimal design of power system stabilizers using particle swarm optimization', IEEE Trans. on Energy Conversion, vol. 17, no. 3, pp. 406-413.

6. Abido, MA & Abdel Magid, YL 1998, 'A genetic-based power system stabilizer', IEEE Trans. on Electric Machines and Power Systems, vol. 26, pp. 559-571.

7. Abido, MA & Abdel Magid, YL 1999, 'Hybridizing rule-based power system stabilizers with genetic algorithms', IEEE Trans. on Power Systems, vol. 14, no. 2, pp. 600-607.

8. Abido, MA & Abdel-Magid, YL 2002, 'Optimal design of power system stabilizers using evolutionary programming', IEEE Trans. on Energy Conversion, vol. 17, no. 4, pp. 429-436.

9. Abido, MA 2001, 'Parameter optimization of multimachine power system stabilizers using genetic local search', International Journal of Electrical Power and Energy Systems, vol. 23, pp. 785-794.

10. Adam Dysko, William, E Leithhead & John O Reilly 2010, 'Enhanced power system stability by co-ordinated PSS design', vol. 25, no. 1, pp. 413-422.

11. Albert J Urdaneto & Nelson J Bacalao 1991, 'Tuning of power system stabilizers using optimization techniques', IEEE Trans. on Power System, vol. 6, no. 1, pp. 127-134.

12. Anderiou, A 2004, 'On power system stabilizers: Genetic algorithm based tuning and economic worth as ancillary services', Ph.D thesis, Charlmers University.

13. Anderson, PM & Fouad, AA 1977, 'Power System Control and Stability', Ames IA: Iowa State Univ. Press, First Edition.

14. Anup Singh & Indraneel Sen 2003, 'A Novel Fuzzy Logic Based Power System Stabilizer for a Multimachine System', International Conference on Convergent Technologies for the Asia-Pacific Region: IEEE TENCON, vol. 3, pp. 1002-1006.

15. Arumugam Jeevanandham & Keppana, GT 2009, 'Robust design of decentralized power system stabilizers using meta-heuristic optimization techniques for multimachine systems', Serbian Journal of Electrical Engineering, vol. 6, no. 1, pp. 89-103.

16. Arya, LD, Varma, HK & Cheshta Jain 2011, 'Differential evolution for optimization of PID gains in automatic generation control', Int. Journal on Computer Science and Engineering, vol. 3. no. 5, pp. 1848-1856.

17. Bayne, JP, Lee, DC & Watson, S 1977, 'A power system stabilizer for thermal units based on derivation of electrical power', IEEE Trans. on Power Apparatus and Systems, vol. 96, no. 6, pp. 1777-1783.

18. Bouhamida, M, Mokhatri, A & Denai, MA 2005, 'Power system stabilizer design based on robust control techniques', ACSEJ, vol. 5, pp. 33-41.

19. Buamed, SM & Shamekh, AR 2002, 'A comparative study between the performance of the fixed gain PID and the adaptive self-tuning power system stabilizers', Int. Conf. on Power System Technology, vol. 2, pp. 1233-1238.

20. Chatterjee, A, Ghoshal, SP & Mukherjee, V 2011, 'Chaotic ant swarm optimization for fuzzy based tuning of power system stabilizer', Journal of Electrical Power and Energy Systems, vol. 33, pp. 657-672.

21. Chatterjee, A, Ghoshal, SP & Mukherjee, V 2009, 'A comparative study of single input and dual input power system stabilizer by hybrid evolutionary programming', World Cong. on Nature & Biologically Inspired Computing, pp. 1047-1059.

22. Chaturvedi, Malik, OP 2008, 'Neuro fuzzy based power system stabilizer', IEEE Trans. on Energy Conversion, vol. 23, no. 3, pp. 887-894.

23. Chi- Jui Wu & Yuan- Yih Hsu 1988, 'Design of self -tuning PID power system stabilizer for multi machine power system', IEEE Transaction on Power System, vol. 3, no. 3, pp. 1059-1064.

24. Chi-Jui Wu & Yung-Sung Chuang 2005, 'Design of decentralized output feedback power system stabilizers using hybrid differential evolution', Power Engineering Society General Meeting, vol. 2, pp. 1404-1411.

25. Ching-Hung Lee, Pei-Yuan Chung & Hao Han Chang 2011, 'A Novel Hybrid Differential Evolution: A comparative study on function optimization', Proceedings of the International Multi conference Engineers and Computer Scientists, vol. 2, pp. 1-6.

26. Chipper field, AJ, Fleming, PJ, Pohlheim, H & Fonseca, CM 1994, 'Genetic Algorithm Toolbox User's Guide', ACSE Research Report no.512, University of Sheffield.

27. Colorni, A, Dorigo, M & Maniezzo, V 1991, 'Distributed optimization by ant colonies', Proceedings of ECAL 91, European Conference on Artificial Life, Elsevier Publishing, Amsterdam.

28. Darwin, C 1973, The Origin of Species, Dent Gordon, London.

29. De Falco, I, Del Balio, R, Della Cioppa, A & Tarantino, E 1996, 'Breeder genetic algorithms for airfoil design optimization', IEEE International Conference on Evolutionary Computation, pp. 71-75.

30. De Mello, D & Concordia, C 1969, 'Concepts of synchronous machine stability as affected by excitation control', IEEE Trans. Power App. Syst., vol. PAS-88, no. 2, pp. 316-329.

31. Dengfeng Xu & Liping Fu 2009, 'Ant colony optimization and its applications', International Workshop on Intelligent Systems, pp. 1-4.

32. Do Bomfim, ALB, Taranto, GN & Flacao, DM 2000, 'Simultaneous tuning of power system damping controllers using genetic algorithms', IEEE Trans. on Power Systems, vol. 15, no. 1, pp. 163-169.

33. Dorigo, M & Luca MG 1997, 'Ant colony system: A Cooperative learning approach to the travelling salesman problem', IEEE Trans. on Evolutionary Computation, vol. 1, no. 1, pp. 53 – 66.

34. Dorigo, M & Dicaro 1999, 'The Ant Colony Optimization: A New Meta- Heuristic', InD. corne, Dorigo, M. and Gloves, F. Editors, New Ideas in Optimization, Mc Graw Hill.

35. Dorigo, M & Stutzle, T 2004, ' Ant Colony Optimization', Cambridge, MA: MIT Press.

36. El-Metwally, KA & Malik, OP 1995, 'Fuzzy logic power system stabiliser', IEEE Proceedings Generation Transmission Distribution, vol. 142, no. 3, pp. 277- 281.

37. El-Zonkoly, AM 2006 'Optimal tuning of power systems stabilizers and AVR gains using particle swarm optimization', International Journal of Expert Systems with Applications, vol. 31, no. 939, pp. 551-557.

38. Febres, AT, Araujo, PB & Furini, MA 2008, 'Damping of low - frequency oscillations by supplementary control of power system stabilizer', TEMA Tend. Mat. Apl. Comput. vol. 9, no. 2, pp. 223-232.

39. Folly, KA & Sheetekala, SP 2010, 'Optimal design of power system controller using Breeder Genetic Algorithm', Bio-Inspired Computational Algorithms and Their Applications, pp. 303-316.

40. Folly, KA 2006, 'Design of power system stabilizer: A comparison between genetic algorithms and population based incremental learning', Power Engineering Society General Meeting, vol. 19.

41. Fraile Ardanuy, J & Zufiria, PJ 2007, 'Design and comparison of adaptive power system stabilizers based on neural fuzzy networks and genetic algorithm', Neuro Computing, vol. 70, pp. 2902-2912.

42. Gegov, A 1996, 'Distributed Fuzzy Control of Multivariable Systems', Dordrecht, The Netherlands: Kluwer.

43. Glover, F & Laguna, M 1997, Tabu Search, Kluwer Academic Publishers, Boston.

44. Goldberg, DE 1989, 'Genetic algorithm in Search, Optimization and Machine learning', Addison-Wesley.

45. Gupta, R, Bandopadhya, B & Kulkarni, AM 2005, 'Power system stabilizer for multi machine power system using robust decentralized periodic output feedback', IEE Proc. Control Theory Application, vol. 152, pp. 3-8.

46. Gurunath Gurrala & Indraneel Sen 2010, 'Power system stabilizers design for interconnected power systems', IEEE Trans. on Power Systems, vol. 25, pp. 1042-1051.

47. Hassan Ghasemi 2006, 'On-line Monitoring And Oscillatory Stability Margin Prediction In Power Systems Based on System Identification', Ph.D Thesis, Waterloo, Ontario, Canada.

48. Hassan, M, Malik, OP & Hope, GS 1991, ' A fuzzy logic based stabilizer for a synchronous machine', IEEE Trans. on Evolutionary Computation, vol. 6, no. 3, pp. 407-413.

49. Hisham M Soliman, Ehab HE Bayoumi & Mohamed M Hassan 2008, 'PSO based power system stabilizer for minimal overshoot and control constraints', Journal of Electrical Engineering, vol. 59, no. 3, pp. 134-140.

50. Hoang, P & Tomsovic, K 1996, 'Design and analysis of an adaptive fuzzy power system stabilizer', IEEE Trans. on Energy Conversion, vol. 11, no. 2, pp. 455-461.

51. Holland, J 1975, ' Adaptation in Natural and Artificial Systems', Ann Arbor: University of Michigan Press.

52. Hong, Ying-Yi & Wu Wen-Ching 1999, 'A new approach using optimization for tuning parameters of power system stabilizers', IEEE Trans. on Energy Conversion, vol. 14, no. 3, pp. 780-786.

53. Hossam EA Taalat, Adel Abdennour, Abdulaziz, A & Al-Sulaiman 2010, 'Design and experimental investigation of a decentralized GA- optimized neuro-fuzzy power system stabilizer', Journal of Electrical Power and Energy Systems, vol. 32, pp. 751-759.

54. Hosseinzadeh, N & Kalam, A 1999, 'A direct adaptive fuzzy power system stabilizer', IEEE Transaction on Energy Conversion, vol. 14, no. 4, pp. 1564-1571.

55. IEEE Task Force 1986, 'Current Usage and Suggested Practices in Power System Stability Simulations for Synchronous Machines', IEEE Transactions on Energy Conversion, vol. 1, no. 1, pp. 77 - 93.

56. Jalilvand, A & Daviran Keshavarzi, M 2010, 'PSO algorithm -based optimal tuning of PSS for damping improvement of power systems', International Journal of Engineering and Technology, vol. 2, no. 6, pp. 556-562.

57. John Greene 2005, 'The basic idea behind the Breeder Genetic Algorithm' Department of Electrical Engineering, Technical Report, University of Cape Town.

58. Kashki, M, Abdel Magid, YL & Abido, MA 2010, 'Parameter optimization of multi machine power system conventional stabilizers using CDCARLA method', International Journal of Electrical Power and Energy Systems, vol. 32, pp. 498-506.

59. Ke, DP, Chung, CY & Yusheng Xue 2011, 'An eigen structure-based performance index and its application to control design for damping inter-area oscillations in power system', IEEE Trans. On Power System, vol. 26, no. 4, pp. 2371-2380.

60. Kenneth V Price, Rainer M Storn & Jouni A 1998, Lampinen, Differential Evolution: A Practical Approach to Global Optimization, Springer.

61. Kirkpatrick, S, Gelatt Jr, CD & Vecchi, MP 1983, 'Optimization by simulated annealing', Science, vol. 220, pp. 671-680.

62. Klein, M, Rogers, G, Moorty, S & Kundur, P 1991, 'A fundamental study of inter-area oscillations in power systems', IEEE Trans. on Power Systems, vol. 6, no. 3, pp. 914-921.

63. Kumar, TKS & Pal, J 2006, 'Robust tuning of power system stabilizers using optimization techniques', IEEE International Conference on Industrial Technology, pp. 1143-1148.

64. Kundur, P 1994, Power System Stability and Control, McGraw Hill Inc New Delhi.

65. Kundur, P, Paserba, J, Ajjarapu, V, Andersson, G, Bose, A, Canizares, C, Hatziargyriou, N, Hill, D, Stankovic, A, Taylor, C, Van Cutsem, T & Vittal, V 2004, 'Definition and classification of power system stability', IEEE Trans. Power Systems, vol. 19, no. 2, pp. 1387-1401.

66. Lakshmi, P & Abdullah Khan, M 2000, 'Stability enhancement of a multi machine power system using fuzzy logic based power system stabilizer tuned through genetic algorithm', International Journal of Electric Power and Energy Systems, vol. 22, no. 2, pp. 137-145.

67. Larsen, EV & Swann, DA 1981, 'Applying power system stabilizers', IEEE Trans . on Powe r Apparatus and Systems, vol. 100, no. 6, pp. 3017-3046.

68. Lefebvre, S 1983, 'Tuning of stabilizers in multi machine power systems', IEEE Trans. on Power Apparatus and Systems, vol. 102, no. 2, pp. 290- 299.

69. Liu, W, Ganesh Kumar Venayaga Moorthy & Donald C Wunsch 2005, 'A heuristic-dynamic-programming-based power system stabilizer for a turbo generator in a single machine', IEEE Trans. on Industry Applications, vol. 41, no. 5, pp. 1377-1385.

70. Lourenco, HR, Martin, O & Stutzle, T 2010, 'Iterated local search: framework and applications in handbook of meta heuristics', 2nd Edition, Gendreau, M & Potvin, JY (eds.), Kluwer Academic Publishers, International Series in Operations Research & Management Science, vol. 146, pp. 363-397.

71. Ma, JT & Lai, LL 1995, 'Application of genetic algorithm to optimal reactive power dispatch including voltage-dependent load models', pp. 5-10.

72. Magdy E Aboul-Ela, Sallam, AA, James D. Mc Calley & Fouad, AA 1996, 'Damping controller design for power system oscillations using global signals', IEEE Transaction on Power System, vol. 11, no. 2, pp.767-773.

73. Mahdiyeh Eslami, Hussain Shareef, Azah Mohamed 2011, 'Application of artificial intelligent techniques in PSS design: A survey of the state-of- the-art methods', Electrical Review, pp. 188-197.

74. Man, KF, Tang, KS & Kwang, S 1996, 'Genetic algorithms: concepts and applications', IEEE Trans. Industry Electronics vol. 43, no. 5, pp. 519- 534.

75. Manisha Dubey & Nikos, E Mastorakis 2010, 'Design of fuzzy logic power system stabilizers in multi machine power system using genetic algorithm', WSEAS Trans. on Systems and Control, vol. 5, no. 5, pp. 312-322.

76. Manisha Dubey 2007, 'Design of genetic algorithm based fuzzy logic power system stabilizers in multi machine power system', International Conference on Soft Computing and Intelligent Systems-ICSCIS-07, pp.214-219.

77. Marco Dorigo, Vittorio Maniezzo & Alberto Colorni 1996, ' The ant system: optimization by a colony of cooperating age', IEEE Trans. on Systems, Man and Cybernetics, Part B, vol. 26, no. 1, pp. 1-13.

78. Marco Dorigo, Biratarri, M & Stutzle, T 2006, 'Ant colony optimization: Artificial ants as a computational intelligence technique', IEEE Computational Intelligence Magazine, vol. 1, no. 4, pp. 28-39.

79. Marsaline Beno, M, Albert Singh, N, Ciba Therese, M. & Mohammed Syed Ibrahim, M 2011, ' Design of PSS for damping low frequency oscillations using bacteria foraging tuned non-linear neuro fuzzy controller', IEEE GCC Conference and Exhibition, pp. 653-656.

80. Martins, N & Lima, LTG 1989, 'Eigen value and frequency domain analysis of small-signal electromechanical stability problems', IEEE special publication on Eigen analysis and frequency domain methods for system dynamic performance', 90TH0292-3-PWR, pp. 17-33.

81. Mendona, A & Pecas Lopes, JA 2009, 'Robust tuning of power system stabilizers to install in wind energy conversion systems', IET Renewable Power Generation, vol. 3, no. 4, pp. 465-475.

82. Michael, J Basler & Richard C Schaefer 2008, 'Understanding power- system stability', IEEE Trans. on Ind. Appl., vol. 44, no. 2, pp. 463- 474.

83. Michalewicz, Z 1996, 'Genetic Algorithms + Data Structure = Evolution Programs', Springer, New York, 3rd (extended) edition.

84. Milad Khaleghi, Malihe M. Farsangi, Hossen Nezamabad-pour & Kwang Y Lee 2011, 'Pareto-optimal design of damping controllers using modified artificial immune algorithm', IEEE Trans. on Systems, Man and Cybernetics-Part C, vol. 41, no. 2, pp. 240-250.

85. Mishra, S, Tripathy, M & Nanda, J 2007, 'Multimachine power system stabilizers designed by rule based bacteria foraging', Electric Power System Research, vol. 77, pp. 1595-1607.

86. Mukherjee, V & Ghoshal, SP 2007, 'Comparison of intelligent fuzzy based AGC coordinated PID controlled and PSS controlled AVR system', Int. Journal of Electrical Power Energy Systems, vol. 29, pp. 679-689.

87. Olof Samuelsson 1997, 'Power System Damping: Structural Aspects of Controlling Active Power', Ph.D thesis, Lund.

88. Osman and Mohamed, M 2006, 'An overview of fuzzy logic based power system stabilizers', 38th North American Power Symposium, pp. 335 - 337.

89. Padiyar, KR 1996, Power System Stability, Dynamics and Control, John Wiley Inter. science Publishing.

90. Pai, MA 1989, Energy Function Analysis for Power System Stability, Norwell, MA: Kluwer.

91. Phiri, A & Folly, KA 2008, 'Application of breeder GA to power system controller design', IEEE Swarm Intelligence Symposium, St Louis, MO, pp.1-5.

92. Pinaki Mazumder & Elizabeth M Rudnick 1998, Genetic Algorithms for VLSI Design, Layout and Test Automation, Prentice Hall, first edition.

93. Pinaki Mitra, Chuan Yan, Lisa Grant, Ganesh K Venayaga moorthy & Komla Folly 2009, 'Comparative study of population based techniques for power system stabilizer design', Intelligent System Applications to Power Systems, pp. 1-6.

94. Ping, H, Kewen, YW, Chitong, T & Xiaoyan, B 2007, 'Studies of the improvement of probabilistic PSS's using single neuron model', International Journal of Electrical Power and Energy Systems, vol. 29, pp. 217-227.

95. Qin, SLD, Jiang, QY, Zou, ZY & Cao, YJ 2004, 'A queen–bee evolution based on genetic algorithm for economic power dispatch', 39th International Universities Power Engineering Conference, UPEC 2004. vol. 1, pp. 453-456.

96. Ragaey AF Saleh & Hugh R Bolton 2000, 'Genetic algorithm-aided design of fuzzy logic stabilizer for a superconducting generator', IEEE Trans. on Power Systems, vol. 15, no. 4, pp. 1329-1335.

97. Ramirez-Gonzalez, M, Castellanos, R & Malik, OP 2010, 'Application of simple fuzzy PSS for power system stability enhancement of the Mexicon Interconnected system', Power and Energy Society General Meeting, pp. 1-8.

98. Reza Hemmati, Sayed Mojtaba, Shirvani Boroujeni & Mostafa Abdollahi 2010, 'Comparison of robust and intelligent based power system stabilizers', Int. Journal of Physical Sciences, vol. 5, no. 17, pp. 2564- 2573.

99. Ricardo V De Oliveira, Rodrigo A Ramos & Newton G Bretas 2010, 'An algorithm for computerized automatic tuning of power system stabilizers', Control Engineering Practice, vol. 18, pp. 45-54.

100. Rivera, DE, Morari, M & Skogestad, S 1989, 'Internal model control for PID controller design', Ind. Eng. Chem. Res., vol. 25, no. 1, pp. 252-265.

101. Ruhua you, Eghbali, HJ & Nehrir, MH 2003, 'An on-line adaptive neuro- fuzzy power system stabilizer for multi machine systems', IEEE Trans. on Power Systems, vol. 18, no. 1, pp. 128-135.

102. Saad Ghaleb Yaseen, Nada MA Al-Slamy 2008, 'Ant Colony Optimization', International Journal of Computer Science and Network Security, vol. 8, no. 6, pp. 351-357.

103. Sabapathi, D, Dhanasekaran R & Lakshmipathi R 2008, ' Design of fuzzy logic based power system stability control for a multi machine system', International Journal of Electrical and Power Engineering, Medwell Journals, vol. 2, no. 4, pp. 248-253.

104. Sambariya, DK, Gupta, R & Sharma, AK 2009, 'Fuzzy applications to single machine power system stabilizers', Journal of Theoretical and Applied Information Technology, pp. 317-324.

105. Saud, A Al Osaimi, Abdel Abdennour & Abdullaziz A. Al-Sulaiman 2005, 'Hardware implementation of a fuzzy logic stabilizer on a laboratory scale power system', Electric Power System Research, vol. 74, pp. 9- 15.

106. Sebaa, K & Bourdour, M 2009, 'Optimal locations and tuning of robust power system stabilizer using genetic algorithms' , Electric Power System Research, vol. 79, no. 2, pp. 406-416.

107. Seborg, DE, Edgar, TF & Mellichamp, DA 2004, Process dynamics and control, John Wiley & Sons, New York, U.S.A.

108. Selvabala, B & Devaraj, D 2010, 'Co-ordinate tuning of AVR-PSS using differential evolution algorithm', IPEC 2010 Conference Proceedings, pp. 439-444.

109. Selvi, V & Umarani R 2010, 'Comparative analysis of ant colony and particle swarm optimization techniques', International Journal of Computer Applications, vol. 5, no. 4, pp. 1-6.

110. Seung - Mook Baek, Jung - Wook Park & Ian A Hiskens, 'Optimal tuning for linear and non linear parameters of power system stabilizers in hybrid system modeling', IEEE Transaction on Ind. Appl., vol. 45, pp. 87- 97. 3

111. Shayeghi, H & Jalilzadeh S 2009, 'Robust PSS design using chaotic optimization algorithm for a multi machine power system', Electrical/ Electronics, Computer, Telecommunications and Information Technology, vol. 1, pp. 40-43.

112. Sheetekala, SP & Folly, KA 2010, 'Power system controller design: A comparison between breeder genetic algorithm and population based incremental learning', International Conference on Neural Networks, pp.1-8.

113. Sheetekela, S, Komla Folly & Om P Malik 2009, 'Design and implementation of power system stabilizers based on evolutionary algorithms', IEEE AFRICON, pp. 1-6.

114. Sheng - Kuan Wang, Ji - Pyng Chiou & Chih - Wen Lih 2009, 'Parameters tuning of power system stabilizers using improved ant direction hybrid differential evolution', Journal of Electrical Power and Energy Systems, vol. 31, pp. 34-42.

115. Sil, A, Gangopadhyay, TK, Paul, S & Maitra, AK 2009, 'Design of robust power system stabilizer using H' mixed sensitivity technique', Third International Conf. on Power System India, pp. 1-4.

116. Sinha, SK, Patel RN & Prasad R 2010, 'Application of GA and PSO tuned fuzzy controller for automatic generation control of three area thermal-thermal-hydro power systems', International Journal of Computer Theory and Engineering, vol. 2, no. 2, pp. 238-244.

117. Skogestad S 2003, 'Simple analytic rules for model reduction and PID controller tuning', Journal of Process Control, vol. 13, pp. 291-309.

118. Soon Kiat Yee & Jovica V Milanovic 2008, 'Fuzzy logic controller for decentralized stabilization of multi machine power system', IEEE Trans. on Fuzzy Systems, vol. 16, no. 4, pp. 971-981.

119. Storn, R & Price, K 1997, ' Differential evolution: A simple and efficient heuristic for global optimization over continuous spaces', Journal of Global Optimization, vol. 11, pp. 341-359.

120. Stützle, T & Hoos, HH 2000, 'MAX-MIN Ant System', Future Generation Computer Systems, vol. 16, no. 8, pp. 889-914.

121. Sumathi N, Selvan, MP & Kumaresan, N 2007, 'A hybrid genetic algorithm based power system stabilizer', International Conference on Intelligent and Advanced Systems, pp. 876-881.

122. Sung Hoon Jung 2003, 'Queen-bee evolution for genetic algorithm', Electronics, vol. 39, no. 6, pp. 575-576.

123. Taher, SA & Shemshadi, A 2007, 'Design of robust fuzzy logic power system stabilizer', World Academy of Science, Engg; and Tech; vol. 27, pp. 8-14.

124. Tridib Kumar Das, Ganesh Venayagamoorthy & Usman, OA Aliyu 2008, 'Bio- inspired algorithms for the design of multiple optimal power system stabilizers: SPPSO and BFA', IEEE Trans. on Industry Applications, vol. 44, no. 5, pp. 1445-1457.

125. Varadarajan, M & Swarup, KS 2008, 'Solving multi-objective optimal power flow using differential evolution', IET-Generation Transmission Distribution, vol. 2, no. 5, pp.720-730.

126. Wang, Z , Chung, CY, Wong, KP & T s e , C T 2008, 'Robust p o w e r system stabiliser design under multi-operating conditions using differential evolution', IET - Generation Transmission Distribution, vol. 2, no. 5, pp. 690-700.

127. Wolfram, S 1986, 'Theory &Applications of Cellular Automata, Advanced series on complex systems', vol.1, World Scientific, Singapore.

128. Wu, QH, Cao, YJ & Wen, JY 1998, 'Optimal reactive power dispatch using an adaptive genetic algorithm', International Journal of Electrical Power and Energy Systems, vol. 20, no. 5, pp. 563-569.

129. Xiao-Rong Wang 2003, 'The Ant colony optimization algorithm based on eligibility trace', IEEE International Conference on Systems, Man and Cybernetics, vol. 5, pp. 4065-4070.

130. Yao Nan Yu 1983, Electric Power System Dynamics, Academic Press.

131. Yassami, H, Darabi, A & Rafiei, SMR 2010, 'Power system stabilizer design using strength pareto multi-objective optimization approach', Electric Power Systems Research, vol. 31, pp. 34-42.

132. Yee, SK & Milanovic, JV 2006, 'Non linear time -response optimization method for tuning power system stabilizers', IEE Proc- Generation Transmission Distribution, vol. 153, no. 3, pp. 269-275.

133. Yuan, SQ & Fang, DZ 2009, ' Robust PSS parameter design using a trajectory sensitivity approach', IEEE Trans. on Power Systems, vol. 24, pp. 1011-1018.

134. Yuan-Yih Hsu & Chern- Lin Chen 1987, 'Identification of optimum location for stabilizer applications using participation factors', IEEE Proceedings, vol. 134, no. 3, pp. 238-244.

135. Yung-Sung Chuang, Shu-Cheng Wang & Chi-Jui Wu 2007, 'Novel decentralized pole placement design of power system stabilizers using hybrid differential evolution', International Journal of Mathematics and Computers in Simulation, vol. 1, no. 4, pp. 410-418.

136. Zhenzhi Lin, Chung, CY & Wong, KP 2008, ' Optimal coordination of power system stabilizers for transient stability enhancement', Australasian Universities Power Engineering Conference, pp. 1-6.

137. Zhou, EZ, Malik, OP & Hope, GS 1991, 'Theory and method for selection of power system stabilizer location', IEEE Trans. on Energy Conversion, vol. 6, no. 1, pp. 170-176.

138. Ziegler, JG & Nichols, NB 1942 'Optimum settings for automatic controllers', Trans. ASME, vol. 64, pp. 759-768.

www.ingramcontent.com/pod-product-compliance
Lightning Source LLC
LaVergne TN
LVHW082334200926
848481LV00012B/3347
* 9 7 9 8 2 3 1 3 6 8 4 9 5 *